IMAGES
of America

SLOVAKS OF CHICAGOLAND

ON THE COVER: The 1918 image on the cover (shown here in its entirety) includes the drama group from SS. Cyril and Methodius Catholic Slovak Church in Joliet, Illinois, that performed the play *Janosik*, the legendary story of the Slovak Robin Hood who stole from the rich to give to the poor. (Courtesy of Jack Hertko.)

IMAGES
of America

SLOVAKS OF
CHICAGOLAND

Robert M. Fasiang and Robert Magruder
with a foreword by Monsignor Joseph Semancik

ARCADIA
PUBLISHING

Copyright © 2014 by Robert M. Fasiang and Robert Magruder with a foreword by Monsignor
  Joseph Semancik
ISBN 978-1-5316-6940-9

Published by Arcadia Publishing
Charleston, South Carolina

Library of Congress Control Number: 2013951281

For all general information, please contact Arcadia Publishing:
Telephone 843-853-2070
Fax 843-853-0044
E-mail sales@arcadiapublishing.com
For customer service and orders:
Toll-Free 1-888-313-2665

Visit us on the Internet at www.arcadiapublishing.com

*To all the immigrants from Slovakia and their children
and grandchildren who showed pride in their heritage and
became good citizens in their adopted country.*

CONTENTS

Foreword   6

Acknowledgments   7

Introduction   8

1.   Old Country: *Starý Kraj*   9

2.   Slovak Churches: *Slovenské Kostoly*   21

3.   Slovak Schools: *Slovenské Školy*   37

4.   Slovak Organizations: *Slovenské Organizácie*   49

5.   Notable Slovaks: *Význační Slováci*   63

6.   Slovak Festivals: *Slovenské Festivaly*   77

7.   Slovak Arts: *Slovenské Umenie*   91

8.   Slovak Sports: *Slovenské Športy*   103

9.   Slovak Other: *Slovenské Iné*   117

FOREWORD

From what is now the Slovak Republic, immigrants came to America in the waning years of the 19th century and the early years of the 20th century. They came from poverty with a yearning for a better life. They brought their faith and often their priests and ministers. They established churches, which enabled them not only to practice their faith but also gave them a means of preserving their culture, traditions, and community.

Robert Fasiang and Robert Magruder have favored us by chronicling the history of these industrious people in Chicago and adjacent areas, such as Joliet and Northwest Indiana. In pictures and commentary, they portray an intrepid group of people who grasped at the American dream for themselves and for their children. Other ethnic groups can find their own experiences mirrored in the toil and tribulations of Slovaks, which resulted in another ethnic group assimilated into the mosaic that is America.

The authors have duly noted the importance of the lodges and fraternal associations, which not only provided insurance to assist with funerals and the care of widows but also were important associations in establishing community and social adhesion for the early years of strangers in a new land.

Woven throughout the texts of the commentaries are the names of Slovaks who became leaders in their communities. Bishop Andrew G. Grutka, born in Joliet, became the first bishop of Gary, Indiana. Dr. Peter Hletko and Msgr. Victor Blahunka were notable figures in Chicago. Peter Visclosky has served as a congressman from the First Congressional District of Indiana for more than 30 years. The mayors of the four principle cities in Northwest Indiana have been Slovaks.

This is essentially a book of pictures with commentaries. Those pictures do us well in noting the dances, plays and dramas, festivals, and Slovak exhibitions that were presented in the Chicago area and in Northwest Indiana.

Slovaks of Chicagoland complements and adds to the other books that describe ethnic communities and neighborhoods in the Midwest. We need to be grateful to Fasiang and Magruder for their work.

—Monsignor Joseph Semancik, PhD

ACKNOWLEDGMENTS

As Slovaks, we felt a need to tell the story of the Slovaks of Chicagoland so that future generations will appreciate the work and timeless efforts of their ancestors.

Thanks to the late Steve Blahunka, who contributed Chicago Slovak Day program books and Immaculate Conception and St. John the Baptist dedication books. Thanks to Jim Vrabel, who searched through 3,000 photographs to give us images of Slovaks for our book. Thanks to Victoria Dieska of St. Peter and St. Paul Lutheran Church of Blue Island, Miss Dolores Macko of Assumption BVM Church in East Chicago, and B.J. Engle of Holy Ghost in East Chicago. Also, thanks to Mary Igras of St. John the Baptist in Whiting and Rev. Arturo Perez of Assumption BVM in Chicago for providing church anniversary books.

Special thanks for photographs from Stephen McShane of the Calumet Regional Archives at Indiana University Northwest and Joe Coates of Calumet College of St. Joseph.

Thanks to John Jurcenko for photographs of Lutheran churches, old photographs, and images of Slovakia. Thanks to Joe Gulvas for his collection of sports photographs and for photographs of himself playing baseball.

Many thanks to the Chicago Bears, Chicago Blackhawks, and Notre Dame University for photographs of their Slovak athletes. Other images came from Joe Fasiang, Ben Skurka, Marilyn Buksar, Phil Mateja, Ruth Banas, Chip Sobek, John Blasko, and Al Fetzko. Thanks also to arts contributors Barbara Mateja Kruczek, Jack Hertko, Larry Rapchak, and Mary Kapitan.

Other contributors were Bernie Pavlovich, Geri Hletko, Marie Pardek Dubec, Robert Shimala, Frank Paunicka, Ray Geffert, Barbara Fayta, Bob Elias Sr., Joe Kovach, Mary Tylus, Fr. John Jamnicky, Msgr. Joe Semancik, Fr. Larry Janowski, Sr. John Vianney, Bob Pastrick, Pete Visclosky, Judy Baar Topinka, Laurene Viater, Veselica, Florence Hovanec, Liz Dedinsky, Becky Coleman, Sr. M. Brigid Fasiang, Vendelin Tylka Jr., Lubos Pastor, Ivan Kralik, the Whiting Chamber of Commerce, Diann's Hair Affair, Peter Banas, Roman Suja, Milan Trandzik, and Rosemary Wisnosky.

Thanks to our acquisitions editor and publisher, Maggie Bullwinkel, for her fastidious and compassionate editorship. Thanks to our families, who provided the inspiration for this book, especially my immigrant parents, Frank Gaspar Fasiang and Barbara Masura Fasiang. Thanks to my wife, Dorothy Fasiang, for all her patience and understanding.

INTRODUCTION

Formerly a part of Austria-Hungary, the Slovaks joined the closely related regions of Bohemia and neighboring Moravia to form the new nation of Czecho-Slovakia in 1918. During the chaos of World War II, Slovakia became a separate republic in 1939 and was tightly controlled by Germany. After the war, communists seized control of the reunited Czecho-Slovakia in 1948 and aligned it with the Soviet Union, which controlled Eastern Europe. With the collapse of Soviet influence in 1989, Czecho-Slovakia became a sovereign state. In 1993, the Czechs and Slovaks peacefully separated. Slovakia joined the European Union and NATO in 2004.

The history of Eastern European immigration to the United States is often overlooked, perhaps because it was so swift and successful. This is especially true of Slovak immigrants. Many Slovaks came to America with few assets and rudimentary educations. Within a generation, most Slovaks and their progeny had achieved, if not exceeded, expectations of success in their adopted country.

The success of Slovaks in America in general and Chicagoland in particular was the result of hard work and dedication. Most Slovak immigrants to the United States were recruited to work in heavy industry. Others sought new lives far from the ethnic and cultural repression of their homeland, then under the control of foreign powers. While many Slovaks toiled in the back-breaking work of heavy industry, others used their wages to open businesses. Slovak Americans opened grocery stores, banks, funeral homes, construction firms, and entrepreneurial ventures.

The first Slovaks came to Chicago before the Civil War and settled in the area near North Avenue and Lake Michigan. They became notable during the Civil War when Col. Geza Mihalotzy organized a militia company named the Lincoln Riflemen of Slovak Origin.

In the late 1800s and early 1900s, vibrant Slovak settlements were established in Chicago, Blue Island, Chicago Heights, Cicero, Riverside, Streator, and Joliet, Illinois. In Northwest Indiana, Slovaks settled in Whiting, Hammond, East Chicago, and Gary. Around the Chicago area, ten Slovak Roman Catholic parishes were established and five more in Northwest Indiana. Along with eight Slovak Lutheran churches and one synagogue, seven Byzantine Catholic Slovak parishes were established in Chicagoland. Several Orthodox Christian churches were also founded by Slovaks.

Additionally, smaller waves of Slovak immigrants arrived after World War I, World War II, the Warsaw Pact invasion of Czecho-Slovakia in 1968 (when border guards unofficially opened the borders to allow people to escape), and the fall of communism in 1989. Slovak immigrants have been about 75 percent Roman Catholic, 15 percent Lutheran, 5 percent Byzantine Catholic, and 5 percent Jewish and Presbyterian.

Illinois has the third largest Slovak population in the United States after Pennsylvania and Ohio. This book pays tribute to the Slovaks in Chicagoland who contributed to the development of their new country. While retaining their culture and identity, Slovak Americans adopted many of the customs of their new homeland. Although Slovaks left their homes overseas, they brought along their traditions in the churches that they built. Slovak Americans in Chicagoland also created cultural institutions and social organizations that both preserved their heritage and helped immigrants adapt to the ways of their new country. For many years, Chicagoland had Sokol athletes and drill teams as well as Jednota Boy Scout troops. The immigrants kept in touch with their own language by listening to the American Slovak Radio Hour on WJOB radio in Hammond, Indiana, from 1931 to 1957, which was broadcast by John Babinec Sr. and Jr. They also read the daily Czechoslovak newspapers, the *Svornost* or the *Denni Hlastel*. The rise of Slovaks in Chicagoland is a tale of American achievement yet to be told. Through the use of photographs, we hope to tell the story of their success and to highlight the wonderful melting pot that is the result. We hope that the ancestral traditions, patriotism, success stories, and legacies featured in this book will serve as an inspiration for future generations to come.

One

OLD COUNTRY

STARÝ KRAJ

The official name of Slovakia is the Slovak Republic (Slovenska Republika), and the national anthem is "Lightning Over the Tatras." Pres. Ivan Gasparovic heads the parliamentary democracy. Slovakia became independent on January 1, 1993, upon the dissolution of the Czecho-Slovak Federation (previously named Czechoslovakia since 1919). Slovakia has mountains in its central and northern regions and fertile lowlands in the southern region. (Courtesy of Slovak Information Center.)

The three stripes of the Slovak flag—white, blue, and red—were established after 1868. The constitution of September 1992 added the coat of arms. The double cross of the coat of arms was originally a symbol of the resurrection of Jesus Christ. The three hills underneath the cross represent Slovakia's three mountain ranges: the Tatra, Fatra, and Matra.

The beautiful St. George Catholic Slovak Church in the village of Bobrovec, Slovakia, was built in 1782. Bobrovec is located in the Tatra Mountains near the border with Poland. Its population is approximately 4,000. (Courtesy of Robert Fasiang.)

This typical Slovak school classroom is on display at the Cathedral of Learning at the University of Pittsburgh in Pittsburgh, Pennsylvania. Paintings of flowers and plants are on the beamed ceiling. The proclamation of the founding of the University of Prague in 1348 dominates the rear wall. On the professor's desk, inlaid wood depicts academic disciplines. (Courtesy of Robert Fasiang.)

At 8,710 feet, Mount Gerlach is the highest peak in the High Tatras and all of Slovakia. This photograph shows the south face of the peak, which is in north-central Slovakia near the Polish border.

The city of Liptovsky Mikulas is located in northern Slovakia. The West Tatras, Low Tatras, and Choc Mountains surround the city. Its major landmarks are St. Mikulas Church, a former county house, and the Meshozy Mansion. (Courtesy of www.mikulas.sk.)

Pictured here at a snow-covered ski lodge in the High Tatras of Slovakia, skiers get ready to take the adventuresome journey down the snowy mountain. (Courtesy of Wikimedia Commons.)

St. James the Apostle Roman Catholic Church in Levoca is more than 700 years old. A functioning cathedral and parish church, it is one of the biggest Gothic churches in Slovakia. It has 15 altars, including the largest and highest wooden Gothic altar in the world, which was carved by medieval woodcarver Master Pavol from Levoca. The monstrances, chalices, and other sacred objects are the works of Baroque jeweler Jan Szilassy and are national cultural monuments. (Courtesy of John Jurcenko.)

In 1780, a fire destroyed Spis Castle, the largest castle in central Europe built in the 12th century. In the second half of the 20th century, displays of the Spis Museum were put in the partly reconstructed castle. Located in the Kosice region near the village of Zehra, it is made of masonry in the Romanesque, Gothic, and Renaissance styles. There are 46 castles in Slovakia. (Courtesy of John Jurcenko.)

The city hall (now a museum) in Bardejov Square dates back to 1505–1511, when it was completed. It is the oldest Renaissance relic in Slovakia. German Saxon weavers founded it in the 12th century. The town of 33,000 people in northeast Slovakia has German roots. It has the best-preserved fortification system, built in the 14th–18th centuries, in Slovakia. (Courtesy of John Jurcenko.)

The three-nave St. Egidius Basilica in Bardejov Square was started in 1427 and finished in 1515. In the Middle Ages, this huge Gothic church was built with donations from wealthy parishioners. The interior has 11 Gothic altars, which represent a small part of 15th-century religious art. (Courtesy of John Jurcenko.)

This is a statue of Ludovit Stur (1815–1856), who in 1844 codified the Slovak language standard that is used today. The statue is in the central square of the walled city of Levoca, Slovakia. (Courtesy of John Jurcenko.)

Msgr. Andrej Hlinka (1864–1938) was a prominent Roman Catholic priest, politician, public activist, and leader of the Slovak People's Party from 1913 to 1938. This statue is located in front of a church in Sliace, Slovakia. (Courtesy of John Jurcenko.)

In 1763, Greek Catholic Protection of the Mother of God church was built in the town of Jedlinka. The three towers consist of the narthex, nave, and sanctuary. Three bells hang in the tower. Cleft shingles cover the church. Divine liturgies are celebrated in the Slavonic language. It is one of 40 wooden churches in the northeastern part of Slovakia. The churches were built without using any nails. (Courtesy of John Jurcenko.)

St. Michael's Gate was built in 1300 in the Old Town of Bratislava. It is the only surviving city gate of the four that permitted entry or exit in medieval times, when fortified walls surrounded the city. In 1758, a statue of St. Michael and the Dragon was put atop the gate. The Bratislava City Museum's exhibition of weapons is displayed in the tower. (Courtesy of John Jurcenko.)

This photograph of a small mountain lake in Slovakia's Lower Tatra Mountains was taken in the summertime. Buildings and roads can be seen along the shore line. (Courtesy of Peter Banas.)

A small steam engine pulls a passenger coach in the wintertime in Slovakia. (Courtesy of Roman Suja.)

An electric passenger train makes a stop at a station in the Tatra Mountains in Slovakia. (Courtesy of Milan Trandzik.)

This is a traditional small home with a wooden roof in Slovakia. The stick fence has a basket hanging on it and a wooden bench in front. (Courtesy of Milan Trandzik.)

This photograph shows a row of small log homes with wooden roofs. They have one or two rooms with outdoor plumbing. Slovak village life was quite spartan in the old days. (Courtesy of Milan Trandzik.)

This small village house with a wooden roof was decorated by its owner. The picket fence allowed the owner to raise a hog or other animals, such as geese or chickens. (Courtesy of Milan Trandzik.)

Pictured here is a farmhouse and barn after a winter snowfall in Slovakia. (Courtesy of Milan Trandzik.)

This photograph shows a ski lodge in Slovakia's High Tatras. Snow is visible on the mountain peaks in the background. In winter, everything is covered with snow. (Courtesy of Milan Trandzik.)

Two

Slovak Churches

Slovenské Kostoly

SS. Cyril and Methodius Catholic Slovak Parish in Joliet, Illinois, was founded in 1901. Until a school was built in 1915, school was held in the church basement. As the church slowly deteriorated, the church was relocated to the parish hall on the first floor of the school building in 1974. The church was destroyed by the wrecking ball in 1976. (Courtesy of Jack Hertko.)

The Grand Arch Mural above the sanctuary entrance of St. John the Baptist Catholic Slovak Church in Whiting, Indiana, was blessed and dedicated on April 27, 1947, the 50th anniversary of the parish. It is the result of study and work by Chicago artist Ludwig Scheuerle. It traces the roots of the Slovak people from Europe to America and to the parishioners of St. John. (Courtesy of Jim Vrabel.)

Located at 4920 South Paulina Street in Chicago, St. Michael the Archangel Catholic Slovak Parish was founded in 1898. It was Chicago's first Catholic Slovak parish. The church was later moved to its present location at 4821 South Damen Avenue in the Back of the Yards neighborhood. While the parish is still active, the school has closed. Benedictine sisters from Lisle (and later Oak Forest), Illinois, staffed the school. (Courtesy of Steve Blahunka.)

In 1906, the St. Joseph Catholic Slovak church, school, convent, and rectory were founded on West Seventeenth Place in the Pilsen neighborhood of the Lower West Side of Chicago. The parish closed in 1968. Rev. John P. Rondzik was instrumental in promoting many parish organizations. (Courtesy of Steve Blahunka.)

Holy Rosary Catholic Slovak Parish was founded in 1907 and closed in 1973. It was located at 108th Street and Perry Avenue in the Roseland neighborhood. The Sisters of SS. Cyril and Methodius from Danville, Pennsylvania, taught in the school from 1915 to 1924. (Courtesy of Steve Blahunka.)

The Catholic Slovak church St. Simon the Apostle, as well as its school, rectory, and convent, was built in 1926. The parish is located in the Gage Park neighborhood of Chicago at 5157 South California Avenue. The Sisters of SS. Cyril and Methodius taught in the parish school from 1928 to 2004. The parish still celebrates a Sunday mass in Slovak. (Courtesy of Steve Blahunka.)

The Sacred Heart of Jesus Catholic Slovak Parish was founded in 1911 and closed in 1990. The church and school were built in the West Town neighborhood of Chicago at Oakley Boulevard and Huron Street in 1916. The Sisters of Saint Francis of Mary Immaculate from Joliet, Illinois, taught grade school from 1916 to 1971. Msgr. Victor A. Blahunka served as pastor from 1921 to 1959. (Courtesy of Steve Blahunka.)

SS. Cyril and Methodius Catholic Slovak Parish was founded in 1914 and closed in 1987. It was located in the West Humboldt Park neighborhood of Chicago at Walton Street and Kildare Avenue. The parish was named after the Apostles to the Slavs, SS. Cyril and Methodius, who brought Christianity to present-day Slovakia. (Courtesy of Steve Blahunka.)

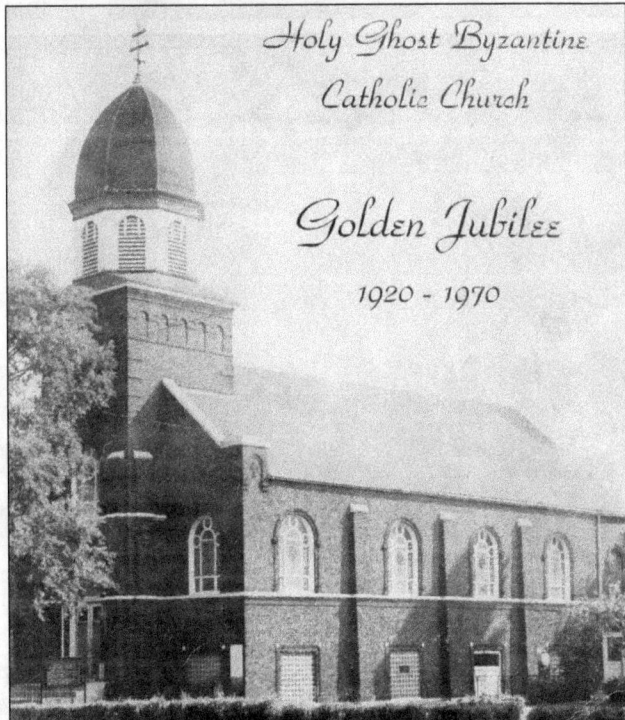

Holy Ghost Byzantine Catholic Church

Golden Jubilee

1920 - 1970

Holy Ghost Byzantine Catholic Slovak Parish in East Chicago, Indiana, was founded in 1920. It celebrated its Golden Jubilee in 1970 with many activities planned by a large committee. (Courtesy of B.J. Engle.)

25

The Assumption of the Blessed Virgin Mary Catholic Slovak Parish in the Indiana Harbor neighborhood of East Chicago, Indiana, was founded in 1914 and closed in 1998. Eight sons of the parish became priests. The parish celebrated its 75th Diamond Anniversary in 1989. The parish grade school opened in 1926 and was staffed by the School Sisters of St. Francis. It closed in 1967. (Courtesy of Dolores Macko.)

This photograph shows the sanctuary of the Assumption of the Blessed Virgin Mary Catholic Slovak Church in East Chicago, Indiana, during the Christmas season. A statue of the Little Flower and the Vatican flag are on the left, the Blessed Virgin Mary is above the altar, and a large crucifix is on the right. Rev. Clement M. Mlinarovich from Slovakia became the first pastor in 1914. (Courtesy of Dolores Macko.)

The cornerstone of the present St. John the Baptist Catholic Slovak Church in Whiting, Indiana, was laid in July 1930 in a ceremony led by Bishop John F. Noll, DD. Pastor Rev. John Kostic, CPPS, ascribed the success of raising $300,000 for the construction the church during the Great Depression to the patronage of the "Little Flower," St. Therese of Lisieux. In June 1931, the new church was dedicated, and the debt was paid off in 1942. (Courtesy of St. John Parish.)

The sanctuary of the SS. Peter and Paul Lutheran Church in Riverside, Illinois, is photographed prior to Sunday services. John Pelikan was the first pastor in 1901. Since December 2000, Dennis Lauritsen has served as the current pastor. (Courtesy of John Jurcenko.)

Located at 91st Street and South Burley Avenue in the South Chicago neighborhood, St. John the Baptist Catholic Slovak Parish opened in 1909 and closed in 1993. The parish never had a school. During World War II, 161 men from the parish served in the US military. (Courtesy of Steve Blahunka.)

Assumption of the Blessed Virgin Mary Catholic Slovak Parish in Chicago was founded in 1903. Until the present church was built at Twenty-fourth Street and South California Avenue in 1914, mass was celebrated at four different sites. The Sisters of SS. Cyril and Methodius taught at the parish school until it was closed in 1916. The school reopened in 1920, and the Sisters of St. Francis of Mary Immaculate staffed it until it closed again in 1985. (Courtesy of Assumption Parish, Chicago.)

Rev. Desideruis Major founded Holy Trinity Catholic Slovak Parish in Gary, Indiana, in 1911. Rev. Charles A. Mosley was its last pastor when it closed in 1997. The Sisters of SS. Cyril and Methodius taught school from 1915 to 1994. The parish celebrated its Golden Jubilee in 1961. Rev. Andrew G. Grutka was serving as pastor when he was elevated to bishop of the new Diocese of Gary in 1956. (Courtesy of Archives Indiana University Northwest.)

This replica of the Lourdes Grotto was built in 1928 on the grounds of Immaculate Conception Catholic Slovak Parish in Whiting, Indiana. The grotto depicts the apparition of Mary, the Immaculate Conception to St. Bernadette Soubirous. (Courtesy of Immaculate Conception Parish.)

The Blessed Mother side altar at St. Stephen Catholic Slovak Church in Streator, Illinois, is decorated for Easter in 2007. (Courtesy of Bob Elias Sr.)

The first Roman Catholic parish established by Slovak immigrants in America was St. Stephen in Streator, Illinois. Established in 1880, Rev. Joseph Kassalko, who arrived from Austria-Hungary, was first resident pastor. The first Slovak school in the United States opened here in 1888. The Franciscan Sisters taught school. A new church was built in 1907, a new school in 1912, a new rectory in 1926, and a new convent in 1958. All Streator parishes have been consolidated to form St. Michael the Archangel Parish, which uses the former St. Stephen church. (Courtesy of Bob Elias Sr.)

St. Peter and St. Paul Slovak Lutheran Parish was established in 1907 in Blue Island, Illinois. This church building that was acquired in 1921 had to be moved by several teams of horses and wooden rollers to its new location on Greenwood Avenue. Church members prepared the foundation. Pastor John Pribula started the first school. Catechism was taught in Slovak. The church was later remodeled. (Courtesy of Victoria Dieska.)

Sacred Heart Catholic Slovak Parish in East Chicago, Indiana, was founded in 1926 and closed in 2011. From 1926 to 1940, masses were held in Eastern-rite churches. The church was built in 1940, at the end of the Great Depression. Fr. Andrew G. Grutka was the first resident pastor from 1942 to 1944. Fr. Joseph Semancik served as administrator of the parish from 1960 to 1969. He returned as pastor from 1974 to 2011. (Courtesy of Msgr. Joe Semancik.)

In 1903, Benjamin and Eva Weiner founded the Orthodox B'nai Judah Slovak Congregation in Whiting, Indiana. These Slovak Jews built the first synagogue on White Oak Avenue in 1910. A new synagogue was built on Davis Avenue in 1950. The congregation closed in 2003. Abe Oberlander served as president for 35 years. He was vice president of the Jewish Federation of Northwest Indiana. He owned the Whiting Laundry. (Courtesy of Robert Fasiang.)

St. Mary's Byzantine Catholic Slovak Parish was founded in 1899, and the parish met in buildings on Clark Street in Whiting, Indiana. The current church was built in 1918; it has been remodeled in recent years. Although the school was closed 40 years ago, the parish remains active. (Courtesy of Robert Fasiang.)

The Henry Schrage house in Whiting, Indiana, was built in 1905. The house and adjoining land were sold to the Immaculate Conception Catholic Slovak Parish building committee for $25,000 in 1925. The house served as the parish rectory until 2000, when Pastor Anthony Ficko died. His first year as pastor was 1983. (Courtesy of Robert Fasiang.)

The Immaculate Conception Catholic Slovak church, school, and convent were built in 1924 in Whiting, Indiana. The school and convent were on the second floor, above the church. The grade school opened in 1926 and was staffed by the Slovak Sisters of SS. Cyril and Methodius from Danville, Pennsylvania. The school closed in 1985. The Slovak Sisters staffed the junior high school from 1940 to 1949. (Courtesy of Robert Fasiang.)

St. Paul's Evangelical Slovak Lutheran Parish was founded in 1904 in Whiting, Indiana. It was the first Slovak Lutheran congregation in the state of Indiana. After meeting in a rental building on Clark Street, a church and rectory were built on Atchison Avenue in 1908. The church was replaced by a new structure, which is shown here next to the rectory, in 1957. (Courtesy of Robert Fasiang.)

The St. Paul Catholic Slovak church, school, and hall were built in 1928 in Chicago Heights, Illinois. From 1946 to 1965, the Slovak Sisters of SS. Cyril and Methodius taught the elementary school students. The school was on the top floor and the hall was in the basement. The rectory was next door and the convent across the street. Rev. Joseph A. Job was the first pastor. Today, most of the parishioners are Hispanic. (Courtesy of Robert Fasiang.)

Founded in 1909, Zion Evangelical Lutheran Slovak Parish held services at the German school at Bickerdike Avenue and Superior Street in Chicago. In 1927, it moved to a church building located at Springfield Avenue and Iowa Street on Chicago's west side. The cornerstone for the present church at 8600 West Lawrence Avenue in Norridge, Illinois, was laid in 1962. Luther Bajus has served as pastor since 1971. (Courtesy of John Jurcenko.)

SS. Peter and Paul Lutheran Slovak Parish was founded in 1901 in the Pilsen neighborhood of Chicago. In 1957, the congregation relocated to Riverside, a near-west suburb of Chicago. The congregation belongs to the Evangelical Lutheran Church in America and the Slovak Zion Synod. (Courtesy of John Jurcenko.)

In 1893, members of the Slovak Evangelical Society organized Trinity Lutheran Slovak Parish in Chicago. Until the congregation purchased a church at May and Huron Streets in 1901, services were held at the German school at Bickerdike Avenue and Superior Street. In 1911, the congregation moved to a new location at Chicago and Noble Avenues. This building served the congregation until 1950, when the present building was dedicated at 5106 North LaCrosse Avenue on Chicago's north side. (Courtesy of John Jurcenko.)

The interior of Trinity Lutheran Slovak Church in Chicago is pictured here. A Slovak language service is held on Sundays at 8:00 a.m. (Courtesy of John Jurcenko.)

Three

SLOVAK SCHOOLS
SLOVENSKÉ ŠKOLY

Pastor Rev. Benedict M. Rajcany is shown with the eighth-grade graduates of St. John the Baptist Catholic Slovak School in Whiting, Indiana, in June 1925. The girls had unusual headwear, and everyone had two diplomas. The Sisters of Providence from Terre Haute, Indiana, taught the students. (Courtesy of Jim Vrabel.)

The first school board of Immaculate Conception Catholic Slovak Grade School in Whiting, Indiana, is pictured here in 1926. From left to right are (first row) Joseph Kasper, Joseph Kusbel, Rev. John J. Lach, John Ruman, Joseph Pieter, and Joseph Pohl; (second row) Steven Blahunka, Andrew Jancosek, John Psikula, Laddie Pohl, John Sevcik, Steven Dado Sr., and Andrew Blasko. The Slovak Sisters of SS. Cyril and Methodius taught the pupils. (Courtesy of Steve Blahunka.)

In November 1926, Immaculate Conception Catholic Slovak Grade School was dedicated by Rt. Rev. John F. Noll, DD, bishop of the Roman Catholic Diocese of Fort Wayne, Indiana. Pictured are the seventh- and eighth-grade students who attended the school at the time. Both grades, 59 students in total, were taught by one nun in a single classroom. (Courtesy of Steve Blahunka.)

This photograph shows the First Holy Communion class of 1930 at Holy Ghost Byzantine Catholic Slovak Parish in East Chicago, Indiana. Fr. Louis Artim was pastor at that time. (Courtesy of B.J. Engle.)

The 1933 eighth-grade graduates hold their diplomas in front of St. Stephen Catholic Slovak Church in Streator, Illinois. Rt. Rev. Msgr. Louis Biskupski (left) and his assistant, Msgr. George Dzurio, are in the front row. In the middle of the Great Depression, the boys wore suits and the girls wore white graduation outfits. (Courtesy of Bob Elias Sr.)

This photograph shows the confirmation class of 1939 at St. Peter and St. Paul Lutheran Slovak Parish in Blue Island, Illinois. From left to right are (first row) Mildred Vankus, Elanor Vankus, Pastor James Sopko, and Vera Yatka; (second row) Don Paska, Matilda Lehocky, Elsie Bartos, Rose Pribula, Bessie Flaskar, Pauline Dieska, Mildred Kutlik, and Julius Pribula. The Rev. James Sopko served as pastor from 1934 to 1939. (Courtesy of Victoria Dieska.)

These happy, smiling, fourth-grade girls were pupils at St. John the Baptist Catholic Slovak School in Whiting, Indiana. They belonged to the "Greatest Generation," which grew up during the Great Depression. There were no lay teachers in those days, so the Sisters of Providence had to teach a class size of 39. (Courtesy of Jim Vrabel.)

This 1940 photograph shows the third- and fourth-graders at St. John the Baptist Catholic Slovak School in Whiting, Indiana. Most of the boys wore ties and some even wore suspenders. The teaching nuns were the Sisters of Providence of St. Mary-of-the-Woods in Terre Haute, Indiana. When they began teaching in 1901, there were 75 pupils. (Courtesy of Jim Vrabel.)

The sixth-grade boys class from St. John the Baptist Catholic Slovak School in Whiting, Indiana, graduated from grade school in 1943. They went to high school at George Rogers Clark in the Robertsdale neighborhood of Hammond, Hammond Tech, Whiting, or Bishop Noll Institute in Hammond, Indiana. (Courtesy of Jim Vrabel.)

St. John the Baptist Catholic Slovak Church in Whiting, Indiana, built the first parish school in 1903. Although the boys and girls were together in first grade, the Sisters of Providence taught them separately in grades two through eight. The tuition was $1 per month for 10 months. An eighth-grade boy ringing a large hand bell announced lunch period and recess. In 1950, a new school was built to replace it. (Courtesy of St. John Parish.)

Pastor Rev. John Kostik, CPPS, sits with the eighth-grade graduating class of 1941 at St. John the Baptist Catholic Slovak School in Whiting, Indiana. The Greatest Generation conquered the Great Depression, and most of the boys were in military service by the end of World War II and the Korean War. The class of 34 boys and 37 girls went to school in separate classrooms after first grade. (Courtesy of Marie Pardek Dubec.)

This photograph shows the eighth-grade graduation class of 1942 of the Immaculate Conception Catholic Slovak School in Whiting, Indiana. In the first row are Pastor Rev. John Lach (left) and his assistant, Rev. James Cis. Some of the graduates stayed for the two years of high school offered by Immaculate Conception. The Sisters of SS. Cyril and Methodius taught the Slovak language to the students. (Courtesy of Steve Blahunka.)

Assumption Catholic Slovak School in the Indiana Harbor neighborhood of East Chicago, Indiana, was erected in 1926. Rt. Rev. Msgr. W. Berg of Hammond, Indiana, blessed and dedicated the school in 1927 (the same year that the School Sisters of St. Francis from Milwaukee, Wisconsin, began to teach the children of Assumption Parish). Three hundred children were enrolled. The four classrooms could not accommodate the entire student body, so some classes met in the church basement. In celebration of the 40th anniversary of the parish, the school was modernized and enlarged with a new recreational center from 1954 to 1956. The cost was $480,000. (Courtesy of Dolores Macko.)

Shown are the trustees and building committee of Assumption of the Blessed Virgin Mary Catholic Slovak Parish in the Indiana Harbor neighborhood of East Chicago, Indiana. Pictured in 1955 from left to right are (first row) Frank Kopanda, Rev. Joseph Semancik, Rev. John Zubak, and Joseph Hlad; (second row) George Poloncak, Clement Tomczak, Anton Ficko, George Spisak, Stephen Bajo, Anthony Ronciak, Peter Matuga, and Gus Badar (committee member Peter Zajac was not present for this photograph). (Courtesy of Dolores Macko.)

Along with the First Holy Communion class of 1968, Rev. Michael Evanick—administrator of Holy Ghost Byzantine Catholic Church in East Chicago, Indiana—stands behind the altar of the sanctuary in his priestly vestments. He is assisted by two altar boys. The boys and girls are holding their prayer book gifts. (Courtesy of B.J. Engle.)

In 1887, Benedictine monks founded St. Procopius College in Chicago to educate men of Czech and Slovak descent. The college moved from Chicago to Lisle, Illinois, in 1901. It became coeducational in 1968 and was renamed Illinois Benedictine College in 1971. In 1996, the name was changed again to Benedictine University. (Courtesy of Steve Blahunka.)

St. Joseph's College was founded in 1954 and began classes in this rented building on Indianapolis Boulevard in downtown East Chicago, Indiana. The name was changed to Calumet College in 1974, and it moved to Whiting, Indiana, in 1976. The name was changed to Calumet College of St. Joseph in 1988. (Courtesy of Calumet College.)

Fr. John M. Lefko, CPPS, (1912–2002) was the first president of St. Joseph's College in East Chicago, Indiana, in 1954. He retired as president in 1975. Father Lefko was appointed assistant pastor at St. John the Baptist Catholic Slovak Church in Whiting, Indiana, in 1938. He became pastor in 1945, replacing Fr. John Kostik. He initiated plans in 1948 to build a new parish school, which was dedicated in March 1950. He left in 1953 for St. Joseph's College in Rensselaer, Indiana. (Courtesy of Calumet College.)

The 1941 eighth-grade graduates from St. John the Baptist Catholic Slovak School in Whiting, Indiana, held their first reunion in 1991, fifty years after graduating. They continued having reunions every five years and started having annual reunions in 2007. In the back row are Msgr. Joseph F. Semancik (eighth from the left) and Fr. John Lefko, CPPS (sixth from the right). Monsignor Semancik cochaired the reunion committee with Robert M. Fasiang (who is in the back row, third person from the right). (Courtesy of Robert Fasiang.)

Calumet College of St. Joseph in Whiting, Indiana, received this building as a donation from Amoco Oil Company in 1976. Fr. John M. Lefko, CPPS, was instrumental in the talks with Amoco to get its former research laboratory building and land donated for educational purposes. (Courtesy of Calumet College.)

This photograph depicts the 2012 addition to Calumet College of St. Joseph in Whiting, Indiana. The addition has a room dedicated to the archives of Slovak bishop Andrew G. Grutka, who was appointed the first bishop of the newly created Roman Catholic Diocese of Gary, Indiana, in 1956. The addition has a lobby and common area. On the third floor are science labs and offices. The statue in front of the new addition is of St. Joseph. (Courtesy of Calumet College.)

Pictured is St. John the Baptist Catholic Slovak School in Whiting, Indiana. In 1950, the old school was replaced by this new building, which was called the St. John Parochial Center. In May 1951, the top-floor convent was completed as well as the Quonset hut gymnasium next to the church. In November 1956, Bishop Leo Pursley dedicated a new wing. It included six classrooms, an auditorium, gymnasium, three meeting rooms, a sewing room, and other utility rooms. (Courtesy of Robert Fasiang.)

Andrean High School in Merrillville, Indiana, was founded in 1959. The Slovak Sisters of SS. Cyril and Methodius from Danville, Pennsylvania, staffed the school. Their religious order, founded in 1909, was named after the two saints revered in Slovakia. Fr. Matthew Jankola, a Slovak-born priest, started the order with three nuns, who were all named Mary. (Courtesy of Robert Fasiang.)

Four

SLOVAK ORGANIZATIONS
SLOVENSKÉ ORGANIZÁCIE

In 1905, Fr. John Rondzik was photographed with members of Branch 493 of the First Catholic Slovak Union. The members belonged to Assumption of the Blessed Virgin Mary Catholic Slovak Parish in Chicago. (Courtesy of Steve Blahunka.)

In 1931, these women were the officers of Branch 225 of the St. Catherine Martyr Society of the First Catholic Slovak Ladies Association (FCSLA), which was founded in 1906. The lodge was based at St. Michael the Archangel Catholic Slovak Parish in Chicago. From left to right are (first row) Emilia Myslewsky, Maria Kobilak, Katarina Bucz, Zofia Trop, and Margaret Holupkovic; (second row) Anna Kovalcik, Emilia Kobilak, Maria Badar, and Katarina Pempek. (Courtesy of Steve Blahunka.)

In 1924, the founding officers of Branch 452 of the Assumption of the Blessed Virgin Mary Society and Junior Branch 348 of the First Catholic Slovak Ladies Association posed for a photograph. The lodges were based at Immaculate Conception Catholic Slovak Parish in Whiting, Indiana. From left to right are (first row) Zuzanna Novotny, Terezia Vasilak, Maria Kalanik, and Kristina Saliga; (second row) Anna Gandy and Emilia Bucany. (Courtesy of Steve Blahunka.)

This is a 1925 photograph of the St. Aloysius Slovak Cadets of the Second Regiment, Company A and members of Branch 485 of the First Catholic Slovak Union in Chicago. They were based at St. Michael the Archangel Catholic Slovak Parish. This was the first Chicago Jednota lodge to sponsor a Boy Scout troop. (Courtesy of Steve Blahunka.)

This 1927 photograph shows the finance committee of St. John the Baptist Catholic Slovak Parish in Whiting, Indiana. Pastor Benedict Rajcany is in the first row, second from the left, and Assistant Pastor John Kostik is second on the right. (Courtesy of Steve Blahunka.)

In 1931, members of the Catholic Order of Foresters, St. Benedict Court 1325, posed for a photograph. The lodge was sponsored by St. John the Baptist Catholic Slovak Parish in Whiting, Indiana. Pastor Rev. John Kostik was the moderator. Rev. Benedict M. Rajcany was the lodge founder. (Courtesy of Steve Blahunka.)

This photograph of Branch 81 of the First Catholic Slovak Ladies Association was taken in the 1930s. The lodge was based at St. John the Baptist Catholic Slovak Parish in Whiting, Indiana. From left to right are (first row) Helena Kocan, Rev. John Kostik, and Sophie Kaminsky; (second row) Anna Kochis, Mary Holman, Mary Molson, Mary Hlavach, Mary Rusko, and Sophie Gresko. (Courtesy of St. John Parish.)

This 1930s photograph shows the Senior Holy Name Society at St. John the Baptist Catholic Slovak Parish in Whiting, Indiana. From left to right are (first row) Jan Lacko, Andrew Fedorko, Stefan Zabrecky, Joseph Biel, John Kresach, Stephen Biel, and Stefan Juriga; (second row) Tony Barilla, Michal Germick, Karol Kostolnik, Joseph Chilla Jr., George Fedorko, Joseph Dolak, and John Pivovarnik. (Courtesy of St. John Parish.)

Florence Hruskovich Hovanec is pictured in her drill team uniform in 1945. The Indiana Girls Drill Team of Lake County, Indiana, was organized in 1934 by members of the First Catholic Slovak Ladies Association, including Supreme President Helen Kocan, Supreme Auditor Anna Hruskovich, and officers from the Gary, Indiana Harbor, and two Whiting branches. The team consisted of 80 girls. A great deal of their success was due to the efforts of James McCarthy, who served as their drill master. (Courtesy of Florence Hruskovich Hovanec.)

Pictured are officers of the First Catholic Slovak Ladies Association Anna Hurban District of Chicago, which celebrated its 20th Jubilee in 1946. From left to right are (first row) Maria Walovich and Maria Osadjan; (second row) Margita Horvath, K. Pempek, Maria Bucz, Bernardina Koscal, and Kat. M. Bomba. (Courtesy of Steve Blahunka.)

The Senior Holy Name Society of St. John the Baptist Catholic Slovak Parish in Whiting, Indiana, is shown in this 1947 photograph. Fr. Edward C. Homco, CPPS, served as the moderator. Their meetings were held monthly after Sunday mass, and a continental breakfast was served. (Courtesy of Jim Vrabel.)

This 1933 photograph shows the ladies who participated in Slovak Day in Chicago, Illinois. This was the 16th annual Slovak Day. (Courtesy of Steve Blahunka.)

With the changes resulting from Vatican II, St. John the Baptist Catholic Slovak Parish in Whiting, Indiana, established its first parish council in the 1960s. From left to right are (first row) William Curosh, Mrs. Joseph Semancik, Mrs. Thomas Ryan, and James LaPert; (second row) Paul Monastyrski, Benedict Danko, Walter Keckich, and Fr. Edward Homco, CPPS. (Courtesy of St. John Parish.)

The Fourth Degree Knights of Columbus, Pope John XXIII Council No. 1696 in Whiting, Indiana, were photographed during the 1960s. The men looked sharp in their tuxedos and bow ties. (Courtesy of Jim Vrabel.)

Holy Ghost Byzantine Catholic Slovak Parish in East Chicago, Indiana, celebrated its Golden Jubilee in 1970. Pictured is the planning committee for the celebration. From left to right are (first row) Mary Pastrick, Mary Prepsky, Mrs. John Sirak, Helen Mindala, Mrs. Nick Michel, Mrs. George Havrilla, Mrs. Edward Olenik, Mrs. Nicholas Mattis, and Mrs. Anna Miksis; (second row) Paul Guiden, George Bodnar, Mrs. Walter Olenik, Mrs. Nicholas Petyo, Mrs. Peter Korba, Mrs. George Bodnar, Michael Holiat, Nick Michel, Fr. Michael Evanick, John Petty, Frank Zudock, George Havrilla, Michael Prepsky, and Nicholas Mattis. (Courtesy of B.J. Engle.)

The Church Council of St. Peter and St. Paul Lutheran Slovak Church in Blue Island, Illinois, was photographed in 1982. From left to right are (first row) Irene Lehocky, Michael Lehocky, Beverly Flambouras, Milan Busha, Jana Mican-O'Brien, and Nicholas Splayt; (second row) John Chlapecka, John Mican, Pastor Mark Van Scharrel, Harold Mislich, and David Splayt. (Courtesy of Victoria Dieska.)

Pictured in 1985 is the leadership of Kolbe House prison ministry. From left to right are Rev. Lawrence Craig, John Nasko, Rev. David Kelly, and Rev. George Brooks. In 1984, Pastor Lawrence J. Craig of Assumption of the Blessed Virgin Mary Catholic Slovak Parish in Chicago started a parish-based prison ministry called Kolbe House. A liturgy was celebrated every Sunday for about 30 persons. The prison ministry's mission of evangelization is motivated by prayers to St. Maximillian Kolbe. By 2003, there were 12 paid workers and 80 volunteers at Kolbe House. (Courtesy of Assumption Parish.)

Fr. Stephen Furdek, an immigrant Slovak priest, founded the First Catholic Slovak Union (Jednota) in 1890. It was organized as a Slovak fraternal benefit society, offering life insurance and religious and social activities. This image from 1990 shows the FCSU Region 7 Centennial Celebration Committee chairpersons. From left to right are (first row) Edward A. Uram, George J.E. Michuda, and Stephen C. Yusko; (second row) Arthur J. Fayta, Shirley M. Uram, John A. Massura, Joseph M. Bugel, Maria H. Harcar, Andrew R. Harcar, and Emery Pesko. (Courtesy of Barbara Fayta.)

The four Slovak ladies pictured here on Christmas Eve in 1994 are members of Branch 452 of the First Catholic Slovak Ladies Association. The branch is based at Immaculate Conception Catholic Slovak Parish in Whiting, Indiana. In front is Liz Dedinsky. From left to right are (second row) Betty Ortiz, Annie Ortiz, and Mary Blake. (Courtesy of Liz Dedinsky.)

Francis Cardinal George, OMI, archbishop of Chicago, is pictured in 2003 with Kolbe House Prison Ministry staff and volunteers. He was there for the Centennial Celebration of Assumption of the Blessed Virgin Mary Catholic Slovak Parish. The parish-based prison ministry started in 1984 and continues today. (Courtesy of Assumption Parish.)

Following the Sunday mass at Immaculate Conception Catholic Slovak Parish in Whiting, Indiana, on October 12, 2008, nuns belonging to the order of the Sisters of SS. Cyril and Methodius gathered for a photograph. From left to right are (first row) Sisters Barbara Sable and Brigid; (second row) Sisters Mary Paul, Cyrilline, and Janet; (third row) Sisters Joanne Marie and Carol Ann. A reception followed in the parish hall. (Courtesy of Sr. M. Brigid Fasiang.)

In 2008, present and former general superiors of the Slovak Sisters of SS. Cyril and Methodius were presented with yellow roses in recognition and thanks for their selfless leadership. In front is Sister Raymund. From left to right are (first row) Sisters Linda Marie, John Vianney, and Pamela Smith. (Courtesy of Sr. M. Brigid Fasiang.)

In September 2012, Branch 81 officers and members celebrated the 120th anniversary of the First Catholic Slovak Ladies Association with a luncheon. The luncheon took place in the Panel Room of St. John the Baptist Catholic Slovak Parish in Whiting, Indiana. In 1892, Anna Hurban founded the organization in Cleveland, Ohio. From left to right are (first row) Margaret Abildua, Marjorie Strbjak, Florence Hovanec, and Donnie Sabol; (second row) Geraldine Tumidalsky, Becky Coleman, Dorothy Hoover, and Annette Markovich. (Courtesy of Becky Coleman.)

Branch 81 of the First Catholic Slovak Ladies Association proudly sponsored the water station for the 2012 Walk for Education to benefit St. John the Baptist Catholic Slovak School in Whiting, Indiana. From left to right are Margaret Abildua, Fr. John Kalicky, Dorothy Hoover, Marjorie Strbjak, Fr. Leon Flaherty, Annette Markovich, and Florence Hovanec. (Courtesy of Becky Coleman.)

The newest member of Branch Six of the First Catholic Slovak Union (FCSU), Cosby Timm, was inducted in a ritual in December 2012. The branch, one of the oldest in the FCSU, was founded at St. Stephen's Catholic Slovak Parish in 1890. The people pictured in this photograph attended a branch Christmas party at a local restaurant. From left to right are Logan Chismar, Jay Timm, Cosby Timm, Megan Timm, Paul Chismar (Branch Six secretary-treasurer), Bob Elias Sr. (president), and Stella Elias (vice president). (Courtesy of Bob Elias Sr.)

The Rev. John J. Spitkovsky District of the First Catholic Slovak Union encompasses Jednota branches in Illinois, Indiana, and Wisconsin. Officers are elected by delegates at its annual meeting, held at the former Our Lady of Sorrows Slovak Benedictine Convent in Oak Forest, Illinois. From left to right are (first row) Barbara Fayta, John Jurcenko, Rudy Bernath, and Dorothy Jurcenko; (second row) Robert Tapak Magruder, Joe Bugel, Bob Elias Sr., Pete Turner, and Mark Fayta. (Courtesy of Robert Magruder.)

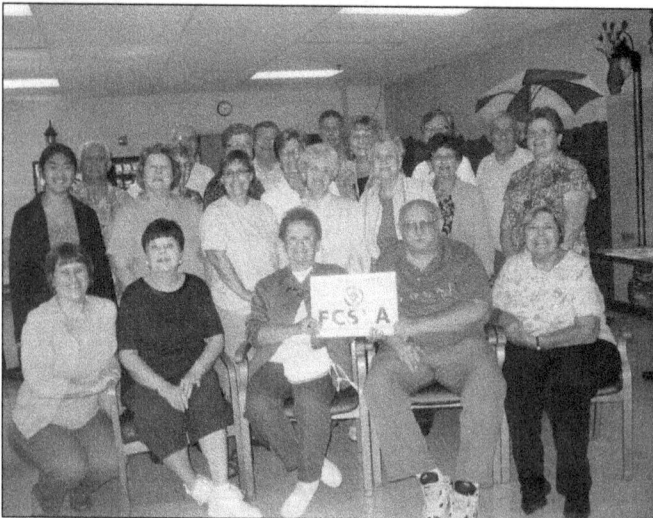

The Anna Hurban Chicago District of the First Catholic Slovak Ladies Association sponsored a Join Hands Day event in 2012. District president Mary Therese Tylus stated that 25 members met in Maywood, Illinois, at the Edward Hines Jr. VA Hospital. Attendees spent the afternoon playing several rounds of bingo with 31 of the veterans. Veterans were able to win some of the $500 in commissary coupons available as prizes. (Courtesy of Mary Therese Tylus.)

Five

NOTABLE SLOVAKS
VÝZNAČNI SLOVÁCI

In May 2012, Rosemary Macko Wisnosky was installed as the honorary consul of the Slovak Republic in Chicago. She assists visiting Slovak dignitaries and other visitors. Wisnosky promotes Slovak activities and assists Slovak nationals with consular needs. Since 1994, she has been a member of the board of trustees for Benedictine University. She is a founding board member of the Slovak American Cultural Society of the Midwest. She has a bachelor of science degree and a master of science from Wright State University.

Slovak Eugene A. Cernan from Bellwood and Maywood, Illinois, was an astronaut from 1963 to 1976. He was the pilot on the Gemini 9 (1966) and Apollo 10 (1969) missions to the moon. In December 1972, Cernan was the commander of Apollo 17 and the last man to walk on the moon, as future Apollo missions were discontinued. He graduated from Proviso East High School and Purdue University and became a naval aviator flying jets. (Courtesy of NASA.)

Dr. Joseph Kovach earned a bachelor of arts degree from St. Joseph College in East Chicago, Indiana, a master of arts in psychology from Roosevelt University in Chicago, and a doctor of philosophy from the Chicago School of Professional Psychology. Since 1984, he has been a professor of psychology at Calumet College of St. Joseph in Hammond, Indiana. Dr. Kovach developed the college's first electronic distance-learning courses. He also modernized his department and developed graduate level courses. (Courtesy of Joe Kovach.)

Author Rudolph F. Kapitan (1929–2006) and his wife, Mary Kasper Kapitan, were married in 1957. They raised two boys and four girls. He wrote his first book, *Seasons of My Childhood*, in 2000 about growing up in Whiting, Indiana. His second book, *Seasons of My Life* (2003), covered the next 60 years of his life. Both books were written in the same true story-telling style. They brought back fond memories. (Courtesy of Mary Kapitan.)

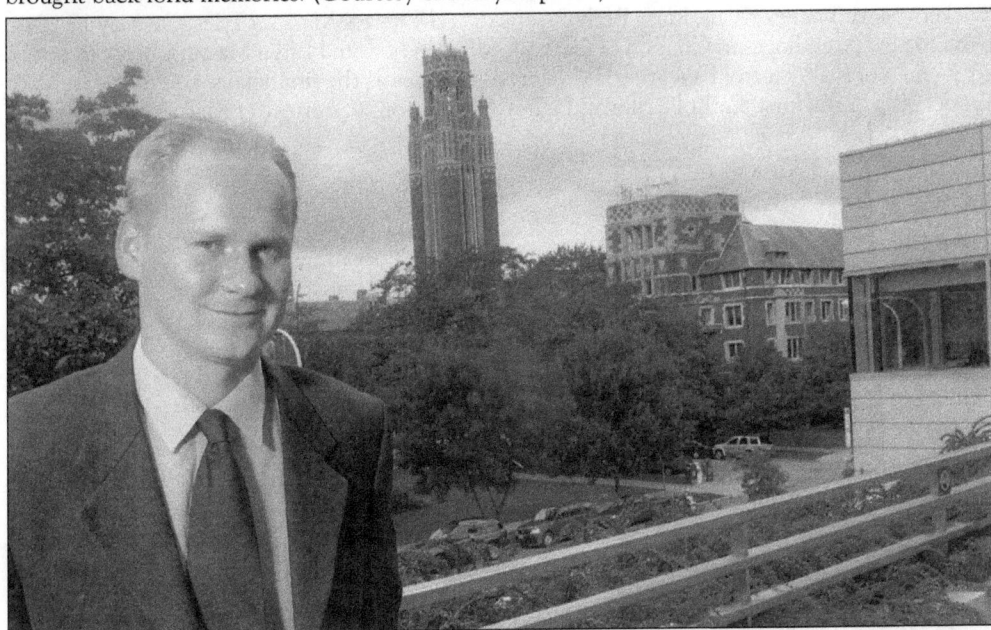

Lubos Pastor, a native of Kosice, Slovakia, is the Charles P. McQuaid Professor of Finance and Robert King Steel Faculty Fellow at the University of Chicago Booth School of Business. He is also a research associate at the National Bureau of Economic Research and research fellow at the Center for Economic Policy and Research in London. Professor Pastor's research focuses mostly on the stock market and asset management. (Courtesy of Lubos Pastor.)

From left to right are Gretchen Gilbert, LuAnn Hoffman, Lydia Massura Berry, Joan Massura Wickers, Mary Therese Tylus, Mary Beth Ossowski, and Therese Massura Tylus. On May 19, 2012, the Chicago Archdiocesan Council of Catholic Women honored Lydia Massura Berry as one of 16 Women of the Year from Vicariate IV. Berry also serves as the financial secretary-treasurer of Branch 485 of the First Catholic Slovak Ladies Association. (Courtesy of Mary Therese Tylus.)

Rev. Msgr. Clement M. Mlinarovich (1887–1971) entered the Franciscan seminary in Bratislava, Austria-Hungary (Slovakia), and was ordained as a priest in 1910. He came to the United States in 1914 and became the founding pastor of Assumption of the Blessed Virgin Mary Catholic Slovak Parish in East Chicago, Indiana. He retired in 1950. He authored 16 books in Slovak. During his 17 years as president of the Slovak Catholic Federation, the organization financed the construction of the SS. Cyril and Methodius Institute in Rome. (Courtesy of Dolores Macko.)

Fr. John A. Jamnicky is the founding pastor of St. Raphael the Archangel Catholic Parish in Old Mill Creek, Illinois, which was established in 2007. He was born in 1945 on the southeast side of Chicago. Educated in Catholic schools, he attended St. Mary of the Lake Seminary and was ordained a priest in 1972. From 1972 to 1981, he was pastor of St. Martin Parish in Chicago. He has served as a chaplain in prisons, hospitals, and airports. (Courtesy of Fr. John Jamnicky.)

Bishop Andrew Gregory Grutka, DD, (1908–1993) was born in Joliet, Illinois, to Slovak immigrant parents. He entered St. Procopius College in Lisle, Illinois, and was accepted as a candidate for the priesthood by the Diocese of Fort Wayne, Indiana. He attended the North American College in Rome, where he was ordained in 1933. He was appointed as the pastor of Sacred Heart Catholic Slovak Parish in East Chicago, Indiana, in 1942 and became the pastor of Holy Trinity Catholic Slovak Parish in Gary, Indiana, two years later. In 1956, he became the first bishop of the newly created Diocese of Gary. He retired as bishop in 1984. (Courtesy of Archives Indiana University Northwest.)

Msgr. Joseph J. Viater's (1930–1996) legacy was built upon social justice. He graduated from Indiana University in 1953 and then served in the Army for two years. He went to St. Meinrad Seminary and the Lateran University in Rome. He was ordained a priest in 1961 and awarded a doctorate in 1964. He then served in many Northwest Indiana parishes and also worked as a prison chaplain. In 1984, Pope John Paul II elevated him to monsignor. (Courtesy of Laurene Viater.)

Msgr. Joseph F. Semancik attended Catholic grade and high school. After studies at St. Meinrad Seminary, he was ordained a priest in 1953. Semancik earned a master of arts in social work from Loyola University in Chicago and a doctorate from the University of Chicago. He was director of Catholic Charities from 1960 to 1998. He was named a monsignor by the pope in 1984. He was the pastor of Sacred Heart Catholic Slovak Parish in East Chicago, Indiana, from 1974 to 2011. (Courtesy of Msgr. Joe Semancik.)

Rev. John E. Kalicky, CPPS, became pastor of St. John the Baptist Catholic Slovak Parish in Whiting, Indiana, in June 1991. He became its third homegrown pastor, after Fr. Gabriel Brenkus and Fr. Edward Homco. On June 10, 1961, Deacon John Kalicky was raised to the priesthood in the Chapel of the Assumption of Mary in Carthagena, Ohio. This is the location of the motherhouse of the Precious Blood Fathers in the United States and the home of St. Charles Seminary. (Courtesy of St. John Parish.)

Fr. Lawrence (Larry) Janowski is a Chicago native, poet, and educator. An alumnus of St. Michael the Archangel Catholic Slovak elementary school, he attended high school at St. Bonaventure in Wisconsin. He earned a master of arts degree from Aquinas Institute of Theology (St. Louis) and a master of fine arts from Vermont College (Montpelier). He professed as a Franciscan friar (Assumption BVM Province) in 1972 and was ordained a priest in 1973. His professional life includes communications, retreat work, writing, and vocation training. (Courtesy of Fr. Larry Janowski.)

Sister Cecilia Kondrc (1911–1985), a Slovak nun from Bratislava, had her story of escape from communist secret police told in a 1954 book, *The Deliverance of Sister Cecilia*. William Brinkey, a reporter for *Life* magazine, authored the article. Claudette Colbert played Sister Cecilia in a one-hour telecast on *Climax Mystery Theatre* in May 1955. Sister Cecilia came to America in 1953 and died in Crown Point, Indiana, in 1985. (Courtesy of Marie Pardek Dubec.)

Sister M. John Vianney Vranak, SSCM, attended St. Simon the Apostle Catholic Slovak Grade School and St. Casimir Academy in Chicago. She joined the Sisters of SS. Cyril and Methodius in 1950. She then attended Marywood University and St. Louis University. She taught school in Indiana and Pennsylvania. In 1976, she served on the General Council of her order. In 1984, she became administrator of Villa St. Cyril. In 1988, she was elected general superior. (Courtesy of Sister John Vianney.)

Andrew S. Kovacik (1916–1988) served as the mayor of Whiting, Indiana, from 1948 to 1954. He graduated from Northwestern University in 1941. While in college, he was employed at Standard Oil and was on the board of education. Kovacik was a master of seven languages. In 1942, he joined the US Army, where he served as a member of the Counter Intelligence Corps for two years. (Courtesy of Robert Fasiang.)

Michael J. Blastick (1905–1969) served as mayor of Whiting, Indiana, from 1955 to 1956. On December 31, 1954, Andrew S. Kovacik resigned as Whiting's mayor to become the Lake County auditor. Michael "Mickey" Blastick, a councilman at the time, was appointed as mayor pro tem at a meeting of the Whiting City Council to fill the unexpired term of Mayor Kovacik. (Courtesy of Robert Fasiang.)

William Bercik (1914–1957) served as mayor of Whiting, Indiana, from 1956 to 1957. A Whiting native, he was extremely active in church, fraternal, and civic affairs throughout the community. While in the second year of a four-year term, he succumbed to a heart attack in 1957. (Courtesy of Robert Fasiang.)

Mary Bercik (1914–1996) served as mayor of Whiting, Indiana, from 1957 to 1964. When her husband died in office, the city council appointed Mary Jancosek Bercik to serve for two years, completing the unexpired term of Mayor William Bercik. Mary Bercik went on to seek and win the mayoral office for the next four years. She had eight children—four sons and four daughters. She attended Whiting High School and East Chicago Business College. (Courtesy of Robert Fasiang.)

Joseph Grenchik served as mayor of Whiting, Indiana, from 1964 to 1968 and 1976 to 1988. He was born in Whiting and attended Immaculate Conception Catholic Slovak parochial school. He attended high school at St. Procopius College Academy in Lisle, Illinois. He enlisted in the US Air Force for two years. In 1947, he was employed by the American Trust and Savings Bank of Whiting. He became active in his travel agency in 1962. (Courtesy of Robert Fasiang.)

Robert J. Bercik (1938–1957) served as mayor of Whiting, Indiana, from 1988 to 2003. Born in 1938 to parents William Bercik and Mary Jancosek Bercik, he married his wife, Jacqueline Hrapchak, in 1960. He attended Immaculate Conception Catholic Slovak Grade School, Whiting High School, and St. Joseph's College. Robert was the owner-operator of Whiting Service Station and served as the street commissioner of the City of Whiting from 1962 to 1974. (Courtesy of Robert Fasiang.)

Joseph Stahura, the current mayor of Whiting, Indiana, has held the office since 2004. Mayor Joe is serving his third term, following five consecutive terms as a Whiting city councilman. The mayor has been married to his wife, Diane (Babinec), since 1976, and they have two daughters. He attended Immaculate Conception Catholic Slovak Grade School and Whiting High School. He went to Lakeland College in Sheboygan, Wisconsin. He worked for over 22 years at BP (Amoco). (Courtesy of Robert Fasiang.)

Peter John Visclosky was born in Gary, Indiana, and graduated from Andrean High School. He has a bachelor of science degree from Indiana University Northwest, a Juris Doctor from Notre Dame, and a master of laws from Georgetown University. In 1984, he won the Democratic primary for the First Congressional District of Indiana and went on to win the general election. He called himself the "Slovak Kid" and gained voters with hot dog dinners. He serves on three House committees and 18 caucuses. (Courtesy of Pete Visclosky.)

Robert A. Pastrick was mayor of East Chicago, Indiana, from 1973 to 2004. He was also on the city council for 12 years and controller for seven years. He attended Notre Dame, Denver University, St. Joseph College, and Indiana College of Mortuary Science. He was a funeral director at Oleska-Pastrick Chapels. He received the Sagamore of the Wabash Award three times. He has seven children, 17 grandchildren, and three great-grandchildren. (Courtesy of Bob Pastrick.)

Judy Baar Topinka has been the Illinois state comptroller since 2011. She served as the state treasurer of Illinois from 1995 to 2007. She served as the chairwoman of the Republican Party and was a member of the Illinois House of Representatives from Chicago-area districts from 1980 to 1995. Judy was born in 1944 in Riverside, Illinois. In 1966, she graduated from Northwestern University with a bachelor of science degree in journalism. (Courtesy of Judy Baar Topinka.)

From left to right are Nelson Carter (chief executive of the Chicago Area Council), Chaplin Fr. William Schumacker (Catholic Committee on Scouting), Lou Gallegos (district executive), and John Jurcenko (St. George Medal awardee). John Jurcenko was the chairman of the Catholic Committee on Scouting for the Chicago Area Boy Scout Council from 1985 to 1990. He received the St. George Medal for the spiritual development of Cub Scouts and Boy Scouts in 1987. He had previously received the Silver Beaver Award from the council. (Courtesy of John Jurcenko.)

From left to right are Dorothy Jurcenko, His Eminence Francis Cardinal George, and John Jurcenko. Dorothy Jurcenko was the first and only Slovak to be president of the Chicago Archdiocesan Council of Catholic Women (1998–2000). Dorothy received the St. Anne Medal in 1976 for the spiritual development of girls in the Girl Scout and Camp Fire programs. In 1979, Dorothy received the St. George Medal for the spiritual development of Cub Scouts and Boy Scouts. (Courtesy of John Jurcenko.)

Six

SLOVAK FESTIVALS

SLOVENSKÉ FESTIVALY

The Slovak branch officers of the Chicago, Illinois World War I Savings Committee sold War savings stamps to its Slovak citizens. The first Slovak Day Festival—held on August 25, 1918, at Chicago's White City Park—generated a donation of $22,000 from ticket sales to the Cook County War Savings Educational Fund. A service flag with 1,012 stars, which represented the Slovak boys from Chicago who served in World War I, was dedicated. (Courtesy of Steve Blahunka.)

The first Slovak Day in Chicago, Illinois, was held on August 25, 1918, at White City Park. Sousa's Band, along with Slovak bands, entertained the 8,000 Slovaks by playing popular selections and ending the program with "Hej Slovaci," the Slovak national hymn, and "America." Soloists and singing societies sang Czecho-Slovak songs. The service flag was dedicated and a patriotic speech was made in Slovak by a colonel. (Courtesy of Steve Blahunka.)

For the 1930 Slovak Day, a parade was held at the Chicago Coliseum in honor of the 50th birthday of Slovak hero Gen. Milan R. Stefanik. Horseback riders, automobiles, and musical bands were in the parade. The Chicago Coliseum was host to the Ringling Bros. Barnum and Bailey Circus. (Courtesy of Steve Blahunka.)

This 1931 photograph shows female participants at the 13th Catholic Slovak Day in Chicago. From left to right are (first row) Maria Hrabina, Anna Korman, Maria Hinko, Anna Simek, Julia Krajcovic, Katarina Chmela, Maria Ciz, and Lory Palky; (second row) Maria Zubo, Maria Hinko, Zuzanna Pitak, Anna Kocur, Julia Trtol, Augustina Novak, Maria Skanda, and Maria Scheller; (third row) Veronika Kalafut, Anna Klein, Maria Wargos, Anna Suhany, Maria Holba, and Zuzanna Kuna. (Courtesy of Steve Blahunka.)

This advertisement from 1943 appeared in the program book of the 25th Slovak Jubilee Day in Chicago, Illinois. It looks like the dancer from the French Follies is a gypsy. The Jubilee Day was held at Pilsen Park in Chicago on Sunday, August 1, 1943. A speaker from the US Department of the Treasury thanked Slovaks for buying US War Bonds and stamps. (Courtesy of Steve Blahunka.)

The celebration for the Slovaks who bought US War Bonds to fund three Flying Fortress B17 bombers was held at St. Joseph Catholic Slovak Parish auditorium in February 1945. The Red Cross ladies were in the front with three model bombers on display. The 48-star American flag hangs in the background. (Courtesy of Steve Blahunka.)

This photograph shows the American Slovak National Day planning committee for 1956. The event took place in July at Chicago's Pilsen Park. Boy Scouts from Trinity Lutheran Slovak Church in Chicago performed a presentation of colors and the Pledge of Allegiance. The president of the Slovak American Charitable Association gave the welcoming address. A soloist sang the American and Czecho-Slovak national anthems. Dancing followed the program. (Courtesy of Steve Blahunka.)

Tom Harmon, the 1940 Heisman Trophy winner who played halfback for the University of Michigan, crowned Elaine Buchko, a Slovak, queen of the Gary Golden Jubilee in June 1956. After 50 years, when US Steel started operations in Gary, Indiana, it celebrated with the International Festival in which many ethnic organizations participated. (Courtesy of Archives at Indiana University Northwest.)

Miss Elaine Buchko, a Slovak who was chosen queen of the 1956 Gary Golden Jubilee, visits the Slovak display at the International Festival in Gary, Indiana. The Slovak ladies displayed some of the native Slovak pastries they baked at home. They also showed off their sewing skills by displaying table cloths, scarves, and wall coverings. (Courtesy of Archives at Indiana University Northwest.)

Two ladies are wearing their traditional Slovak folk dresses, known as *kroj*, at the 1956 International Festival held in Gary, Indiana. Also on display are Slovak dolls, ceramic dishes, decorated plates, paintings, scarves, towels, and table cloths. Slovak pastries are on the table, ready for sampling. (Courtesy of Archives at Indiana University Northwest.)

Holy Trinity Catholic Slovak Parish in Gary, Indiana, celebrated its Golden Jubilee in 1961. Gary Bishop Andrew Grutka was the main celebrant of the Golden Jubilee mass at the church. Bishop Grutka was serving as pastor of Holy Trinity when he was appointed the first bishop of the newly created Diocese of Gary in 1956. (Courtesy of Archives at Indiana University Northwest.)

Holy Trinity Catholic Slovak Parish dancers perform at the Golden Jubilee celebration in Gary, Indiana, in 1961. They wore traditional Slovak folk dresses as they sang Slovak songs and danced on stage. While they listened to the piano accompaniment, the audience appreciated the singing and dancing of the parish's young women. (Courtesy of Archives at Indiana University Northwest.)

Venetian Nights on Lake Michigan in Chicago had a decorated boat parade in 1968. Five Slovaks— two men and three women—wore traditional Slovak folk costumes (kroj) on the Slovakia boat. The Slovakia boat was decorated with strings of lights and pennants. The evening's festivities ended with a fireworks display. Antonia Kralik and Anna Ondrus were two of the people on the boat. (Courtesy of Ivan Kralik.)

Northwest Indiana Slovaks celebrate an annual Slovak Day, usually in July, at the Salvatorian Fathers Our Lady of Czestochowa Shrine. The day begins with mass and is followed by a taste of Slovakia from vendors, a performance by Slovak folk dancers, a raffle, and dancing to a local band. (Courtesy of Barbara Fayta.)

In 1989, the Pirohi Makers from St. John the Baptist Catholic Slovak Parish in Whiting, Indiana, took part in the centennial celebration of the founding of the city of Whiting. They sponsored a float in the annual Fourth of July parade, which went down Indianapolis Boulevard to 119th Street and on to Whiting Park on the Lake Michigan waterfront. (Courtesy of St. John Pirohi Makers.)

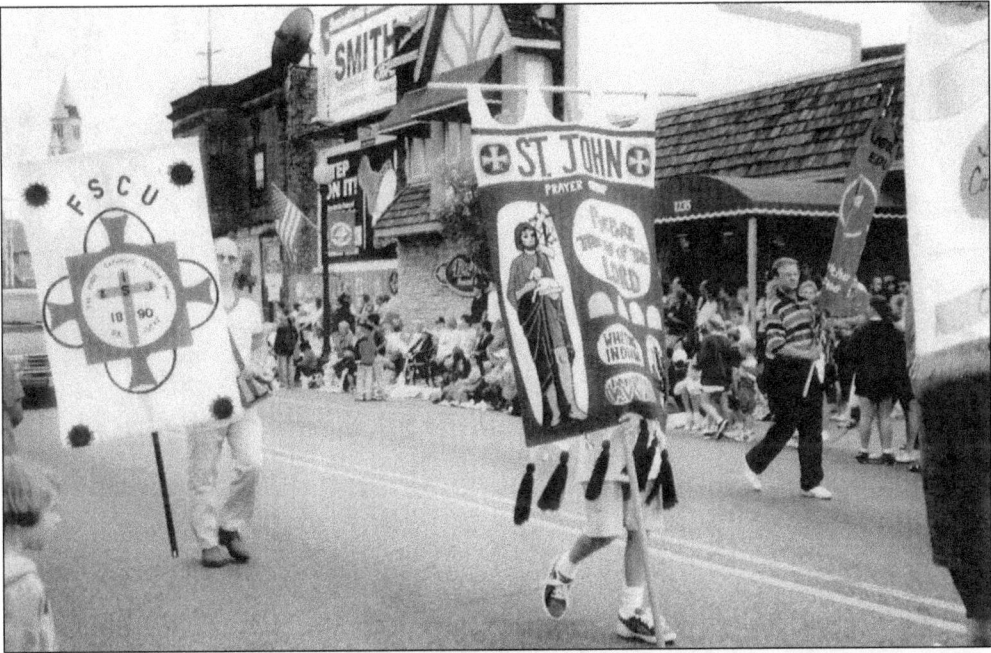

St. John the Baptist Catholic Slovak Parish in Whiting, Indiana, celebrated its centennial in 1997. Different groups from the parish marched in that year's Fourth of July parade in Whiting. In 1890, immigrant Slovak men residing in Whiting organized Branch No. 130 of the First Catholic Slovak Union (Jednota). They twice petitioned the bishop in Fort Wayne, Indiana, for a Slovak priest to found a parish for 50 prospective parishioners. When Rev. Benedict Rajcany arrived from Austria-Hungary in 1897, he became the first pastor of St. John the Baptist. (Courtesy of St. John Parish.)

Assumption of the Blessed Virgin Mary Catholic Slovak Parish in Chicago, Illinois, celebrated 100 years of ministry in 2003. Francis Cardinal George, OMI, the archbishop of Chicago, and Slovak parishioners stand behind the Slovak flag. The early Slovak leaders were Fr. Aloiz Kollar (first parish administrator) and Fr. Peter Kloss (first pastor) as well as Benedictine Fathers from St. Procopius. Fraternal groups, such as the Jednota and FCSLA, helped raise money to build the church in 1914. (Courtesy of Assumption Parish.)

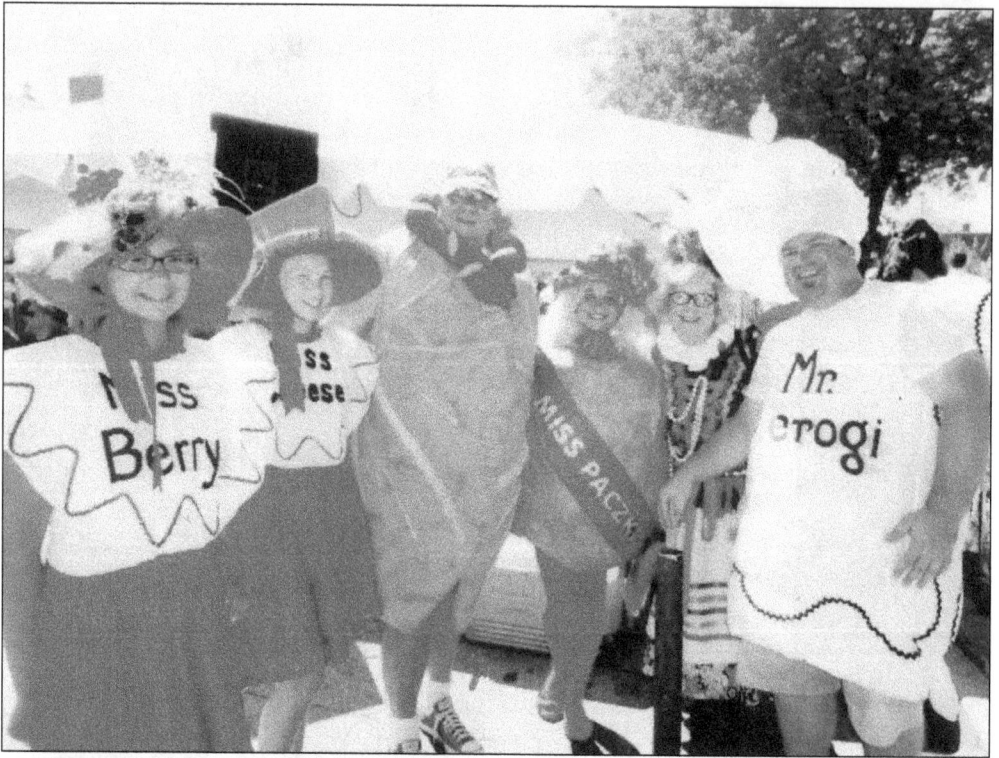

This photograph depicts, from left to right, two Pierogettes, Halupki Guy, Miss Paczki, Polkahauntus, and Mr. Pierogi during the 2013 Pierogi Fest in Whiting, Indiana. Every year, many of the same people play the same characters at the annual Pierogi Fest, held the last weekend of July in Whiting, Indiana. On Friday night, a parade takes place on 119th Street. (Courtesy of Whiting Chamber of Commerce.)

In 2011, ethnic Slovak dancers performed at the Pierogi Fest in Whiting, Indiana. Many of the 250,000 people who attended the 2011 Pierogi Fest saw these ethnic Slovak dancers performing a dance number inside a round, bowl-like enclosure. The dance simulates grape crushing to make wine. The dancers were members of the Veselica Slovak Folk Dance Ensemble of Chicago, Illinois. The boots would keep a grape crusher's feet dry. (Courtesy of Whiting Chamber of Commerce.)

Pictured here are (old grandmothers) at the 2013 Pierogi Fest in Whiting, Indiana. These local Slovaks are wearing babushkas and aprons like women from the old country did. They are holding colorful pom-poms. (Courtesy of Whiting Chamber of Commerce.)

This photograph depicts participants in Whiting's Pierogi Fest polka contest in 2013. The lady with the babushka and her young gentleman partner look like they have a good chance of winning. (Courtesy of Whiting Chamber of Commerce.)

A fiddle player for the Veselica Slovak Folk Dance Ensemble of Chicago plays for children dressed in native costumes. One of the few Slovak folk ensembles in the United States, leader and director Zuzana Fidrikova founded it in 1999. About 27 members dance with the group. (Courtesy of Veselica.)

Slovak men of the Veselica Slovak Folk Dance Ensemble of Chicago gather together to discuss what they can perform in their native costumes at their next performance. The adults practice twice a week at the Slovak Athletic Association. (Courtesy of Veselica.)

An adult member of the Veselica Slovak Folk Ensemble of Chicago happily holds two young girls who will become future members of this group. They perform Slovak folk dances at Slavic festivals and parades all over the Chicagoland area and the Midwest. (Courtesy of Veselica.)

These beautiful young ladies are listening to Slovak music played by the musicians of the Veselica Slovak Folk Dance Ensemble of Chicago. They are under the musical direction of Pavel Melich, who brings numerous years of experience and talent from performing in various folk ensembles around Slovakia. (Courtesy of Veselica.)

The St. John the Baptist Catholic Slovak elementary school band from Whiting, Indiana, marches in the Fourth of July parade in Whiting. Behind the band's banner, two color guards with imitation rifles accompany two American flags and the Indiana state flag. (Courtesy of Jim Vrabel.)

Standing at attention, the St. John the Baptist Catholic School band and drill team is ready to march down Indianapolis Boulevard during Whiting, Indiana's largest parade of the year, the Fourth of July parade. The 50-plus children look sharp with orange sashes around their waists. (Courtesy of Jim Vrabel.)

Seven

SLOVAK ARTS

SLOVENSKÉ UMENIE

This 1915 photograph shows the Holy Trinity Society of SS. Cyril and Methodius Catholic Slovak Parish in Joliet, Illinois, with the Slovak military band in front of the church. While the members are wearing ribbons on their suits, the officers in the front row are wearing sashes. (Courtesy of Jack Hertko.)

These are members of the Tatra Film Corporation in Chicago during the 1920s. They produced a movie in the 1930s titled *Janosik*, which was the story of the legendary Slovak Robin Hood who robbed the rich to give to the poor. This story was also played out on the stage in places like the Slovak Dom in Whiting, Indiana. (Courtesy of Steve Blahunka.)

This 1910 photograph shows the Slovak Sokol men's honor guard and women's drill team, Dejiny Sboru Lodge 51, which performed at Tyler Park in Joliet, Illinois. (Courtesy of Jack Hertko.)

In 1942, the dramatic group from SS. Cyril and Methodius Catholic Slovak Church in Joliet, Illinois, put on the Slovak play *The Wedding*. In Slovakia, the tradition is for the wedding celebration to last all night until dawn. (Courtesy of Jack Hertko.)

This is a Slovak Dance from *Europe in America*, an International Institute program that was given at the YMCA hut in Gary, Indiana, in 1920. Eight foreign nationalities participated, and about 500 people were in the audience. (Courtesy of Archives Indiana University Northwest.)

With Reverend Sindelar directing, the St. Procopius College Orchestra No. 1, from Lisle, Illinois, appeared at the Whiting Community Center in November 1926. The dedication of the new Slovak Immaculate Conception Catholic Church and School in Whiting, Indiana, also had the Notre Dame Quartet and singing schoolchildren on the program. (Courtesy of Steve Blahunka.)

This 1926 photograph shows Immaculate Conception Catholic's Slovak parish choir. Rev. John Lach was the pastor (front row, fourth from the left) and the organist and director was John R. Drac (front row, fourth from the right). They sang at the parish's dedication mass for the new church and school in November 1926. That evening, they also sang during the program in the auditorium of the Whiting Community Center. (Courtesy of Steve Blahunka.)

This 1929 photograph shows the St. Joseph Catholic Slovak Parish of Chicago adult choir and the Reverend John P. Rondzik (pastor). Paulina Sadecky was the organist. Besides singing at Sunday mass, the choir presented several concerts during the year. They sang Slovak songs as well as English songs. (Courtesy of Steve Blahunka.)

A play in the Slovak language about *Janosik*, the Slovak Robin Hood, was performed in the 1930s at the Slovak Dom in Whiting, Indiana. The play was held in the building's top-floor auditorium. Audience members sat in wooden folding chairs. In front of the stage, a fire curtain with advertisements on it was raised just before the play began. (Courtesy of Steve Blahunka.)

Under the direction of Fr. Irenaeus Dolhy, Holy Ghost Byzantine Catholic Slovak Parish in East Chicago, Indiana, had carol singers in 1934. The carol singers visited parishioners' homes after Christmas to sing carols. They brought a model of a Byzantine Catholic church along on their home visits. (Courtesy of B.J. Engle.)

This photograph depicts a 1936 Slovak play at Holy Ghost Byzantine Catholic Slovak Church in East Chicago, Indiana. It was during this time, 1935–1940, that Rev. Andrew Kertis first became the parish administrator before becoming the pastor. Volunteer performers and stage crew performed many plays, which served as a good fundraiser, during the Great Depression. (Courtesy of B.J. Engle.)

This 1930 photograph shows members of the Holy Ghost Byzantine Catholic Slovak Parish church choir of East Chicago, Indiana. Rev. Louis Artim was the pastor at that time. The choir was quite large, with 46 members that sang at Sunday services as well as special concerts. (Courtesy of B.J. Engle.)

Girls from St. John the Baptist Catholic Slovak School in Whiting, Indiana, dressed as gypsies in 1942. They were performing in a school play that was held in the old church gymnasium. (Courtesy of Jim Vrabel.)

James La Pert was the director of the St. John's Drama Club at St. John the Baptist Catholic Slovak Parish in Whiting, Indiana. He started directing in 1926 with the presentation of *Mammy's Lil Wild Rose*. He formed St. John's Drama Club in 1928. It later evolved into the Marian Theatre Guild. James La Pert directed more than 60 plays over the years. (Courtesy of Robert Fasiang.)

A longtime member of the drama club, noted throughout the Calumet Region for his Hollywood-like makeup artistry, John Geffert was overwhelmingly elected to the presidency of St. John's Drama Club in 1945. Almost immediately, Geffert introduced an efficient stock company organization into the active club. (Courtesy of Robert Fasiang.)

From left to right are (first row) Freddie Opat, Ted Molson, Lorraine Kosior and Richard Geffert; (second row) Richard Kaminsky and Joseph Tomko. They comprised the scenic department of the St. John's Drama Club for the play *Good News*, which was performed in November 1946 at the Whiting Community Center. The 1946 second performance was in memory of Bill Spilly, who was the star of the first performance in 1940. He was killed while serving in the Army during World War II. (Courtesy of Robert Fasiang.)

St. John the Baptist Catholic Parish's band is photographed in 1931 in front of the old church in Whiting, Indiana. The Slovak band performed concerts and marched in parades, including the Fourth of July parade. (Courtesy of Jim Vrabel.)

Mike Rapchak, "Dean of the Big Bands," was born in 1920 to Slovak immigrant parents in Whiting, Indiana. He became a radio disc jockey in 1948. He interviewed jazz musicians at WAAF Chicago from 1951 to 1958. He was photographed in February 1955 while doing a promotion. In 1958, he switched to WCFL; he remained there until 1965, when he went to WLS television. He went back to WCFL from 1978 to 1980, when he moved to WGN. He left WGN in 1995. (Courtesy of Larry Rapchak.)

Pictured is the 1982 choir of St. Peter and St. Paul Lutheran Slovak Church in Blue Island, Illinois. Interim pastor Martin Oygaard, a past conductor of the Oslo Symphony Orchestra, began the present church choir in 1947. For many years, the choir was under the direction of Robert Facko. Marilyn Dorcic has served as director for approximately 10 years, during which time the choir has maintained a membership of around 16. The choir also sings at area nursing homes and carols in the homes of elderly members. (Courtesy of Victoria Dieska.)

1st Row: Deborah L. Delinck, Betty Delinck, Jennifer Delinck, Vera Joan Straker, Fran M. Ritzi, Anne Marie Gyure, Anne Zajac, Mary Therese Mundo, Alma R. Koch, Linda Reichert, Mary R. Mores. 2nd Row: Elaine Badnarik, Gerri Tumidalsky, Mary Grenchik, Rebecca Ann Zunac, Marge Tkach, Mary Ann Rosinski, Dorothy R. Hoover, Elizabeth M. Furiak. 3rd Row: John Badnarik, Margaret Saliga, Mr. Joseph Christ, Charles Reichert, Anne M. Kovach, Theodore J. Molson, Thomas Kremaric, Br. Jerry Hall, C.PP.S. 4th Row: Richard Rosinski, Norbert P. Grenchik, Frank Delinck, Charles R. Kovach, Jeffrey A. Delinck, Wendell Klen, George Saliga, Martin A. Dybel, David J. Rohr. Absent at time of picture: Jerry Bobos, Diane J. Kovach, Donna Lewandowski, Jean Poulos, Dolores Tobias, Joyce A. Wagner.

Under the direction of Faith Tumidalsky (now Faith Pratt), with Bro. Benjamin Basile, CPPS, as organist, the adult choir of St. John the Baptist Catholic Slovak made a record titled *Alleluia! Christ is Born* in 1983. Thirty-six choir members of the Whiting church are pictured (eight were absent). (Courtesy of Robert Fasiang.)

Dolores Macko was the organist and sacristan at the Assumption of the Blessed Virgin Mary Catholic Slovak Church in the Indiana Harbor section of East Chicago, Indiana, from 1962 to 1998, when the parish closed. In 2002, she became the organist at St. Patrick's Catholic Church in East Chicago. (Courtesy of Dolores Macko.)

In the first row is Mark Kruczek (third person from the right), the artistic director and conductor of the Chorus Angelorum. He founded Chorus Angelorum in 1985, and the talented group of volunteers performs annually in October at venues in Northwest Indiana. In 2004, he received the Hammond Achievement Award. He is also the featured organist and pianist with the Voices of Ascension Chorus in New York City. (Courtesy of Barbara Mateja Kruczek.)

Mark Kruczek, the artistic director of Chorus Angelorum, is a native of Whiting, Indiana. He has been the music director at St. Joan of Arc Catholic Church in New York City for more than 30 years. At 13 years of age, he attended the pre-college division of DePaul University. He went on to study at the Catholic University of America in Washington, DC, and the Juilliard School in New York. (Courtesy of Barbara Mateja Kruczek.)

Eight

SLOVAK SPORTS
SLOVENSKÉ ŠPORTY

The above basketball players represented St. John the Baptist Catholic Slovak Parish in Whiting, Indiana, during the 1932–1933 season. Moderator Fr. Cyril Ernest is standing on the right. Sports were important for the physical and mental development of Slovak men, even though many were unemployed in the middle of the Great Depression. (Courtesy of Jim Vrabel.)

This image shows the 12 amateur baseball players that were on a team representing St. John the Baptist Catholic Slovak Parish in Whiting in the 1930s. Not only did they play teams from other parishes but also teams representing the oil and steel industries and other manufacturers. (Courtesy of Jim Vrabel.)

This is the 1937–1938 professional basketball team sponsored by Ciesar Auto Dealership in Whiting, Indiana. The team was called Whiting's Ciesar All-Americans of the National Basketball League, and they played their home games at the Hammond Civic Center. Young John Wooden is the fourth person from the right. His nickname is the "Wizard of Westwood." He won 10 NCAA national championships as head coach at UCLA. His team won 88 consecutive games. He was a chosen six-time national coach of the year. (Courtesy of Jim Vrabel.)

Pictured is the 1940 men's basketball team at St. John the Baptist Catholic Slovak Parish in Whiting, Indiana. Moderator Fr. Stephen Tstar is standing at the right in the top row, and coach Andy Vrabel is at the left. Their nickname was the Blue Jays, and their colors were blue and gold. (Courtesy of Jim Vrabel.)

William "Bill" Rapchak played basketball for George Rogers Clark High School in Hammond, Indiana, from 1942 to 1944. He was the leading scorer on the team and ranked number two in the state in 1944. He went to Michigan State University and established the single-game scoring record. He became the Michigan State all-time leading scorer in 1950. He was inducted into the Indiana Basketball Hall of Fame in 2003. (Courtesy of Robert Fasiang.)

Walter (Wally) Joseph Ziemba was all-state in football, basketball, and track at Hammond High School. In 1939, he went to Notre Dame University and earned All-American honors as a center/linebacker in football. He played in the Chicago All-Star Game. Ziemba was the assistant line coach at Notre Dame for 10 years. He contributed to four national football championships: 1943, 1946, 1947, and 1949. He was inducted into the Indiana Football Hall of Fame in 1976. (Courtesy of University of Notre Dame.)

This photograph shows the eighth-grade boys' basketball team of 1944–1945 at St. John the Baptist Catholic Slovak School in Whiting, Indiana. The team won two trophies. The boys belonged to the Junior Holy Name Society. From left to right are (first row) Joe Fasiang, Ed Svitek, Fr. Louis Telegdy (moderator), Paul Hmurovic (coach), Bernie Dubeck, and Gilbert Brindley; (second row) Jim Vrabel, Ed Mores, Al Kovalcik, Jim Figler, Don Vrabel, and Bob Drach. (Courtesy of Joe Fasiang.)

From left to right are Ben Skurka, Bob Strisko, Don Geffert, and Art Gasenica. They were members of Whiting's Slovak Catholic Sokol Assembly 111 track team in 1948. They participated in the running events at the 1947 Slet, which was held at Soldier Field in Chicago. Ben Skurka, a longtime member of the Slovak Catholic Sokol, participated in track events all over the United States. (Courtesy of Ben Skurka.)

"Handy" Andy Pafko, also known as "Pruschka," played center field for the Chicago Cubs from 1943 to 1946 and third base from 1947 to 1951. He was traded to the Brooklyn Dodgers in 1951. He was traded again to the Milwaukee Braves in 1953, and he ended his baseball career in 1959. He played in four World Series and was an All-Star five times. In 2000, Pafko was named to the Cubs All-Century team. (Courtesy of Robert Fasiang.)

This photograph shows the 1948–1949 eighth-grade basketball team at St. John the Baptist Catholic Slovak School in Whiting, Indiana. From left to right are (first row) Andy Gabor, John Petkovich, Rev. Louis Telegdy (moderator), Tom Fasiang, and Joe Hajduch; (second row) Dick Girman, Bob Varshal, Ralph McCampbell, Edward Pramuk, John Stasny, Julius Mikoshy, and Joe Gulvas (coach). Even though they did not win a trophy, they played with a lot of effort and school spirit. (Courtesy of Joe Gulvas.)

The 1949 football team from St. John the Baptist Catholic Slovak School in Whiting, Indiana, is pictured here. This team was coached by Andy Baran (third row, second from the right) and Joe Gulvas (third row, first on the right.) Fr. Louis Telegdy served as moderator. This was the last football team to represent the old school; a new school replaced it in 1950. (Courtesy of Joe Gulvas.)

Joe W. Gulvas played football, basketball, baseball, and track for George Rogers Clark High School in Hammond, Indiana, and graduated in 1947. He played amateur baseball for St. John the Baptist Catholic Slovak Parish from 1946 to 1948. In 1949, he signed to play professional baseball with the Brooklyn Dodgers' minor league team in Danville, Illinois. Then, he moved to Kansas to play for the Hutchison Elks. In 1950, he played with the Vincennes Citizens and later with the Greenwood Dodgers. He was drafted during the Korean War and stationed at Fort Eustis, Virginia, where he played baseball in 1951 and 1952. Willie Mays was on Gulvas's team in 1952; he took Gulvas's place in center field, moving him to third base. After discharge from the Army in 1953, Gulvas played baseball with the Thomasville Dodgers, Santa Barbara Dodgers, and finally with the Miami Sun Sox. (Both, courtesy of Joe Gulvas.)

George Buksar played football, basketball, baseball, and track at George Rogers Clark High School in Hammond, Indiana. After being all-state in football in 1943 and 1944, he graduated in 1945. Before transferring to the University of San Francisco, where he played football and basketball, Buskar played football for two years at Purdue University. He started playing professional football in 1949 with the Los Angeles Rams and then the Chicago Hornets, Baltimore Colts, and the Washington Redskins. Buksar retired in 1954 and was inducted into the Indiana Football Hall of Fame in 2000. (Courtesy of Marilyn Buksar.)

The eighth-grade boys basketball team from St. John the Baptist Catholic Slovak School in Whiting, Indiana, played during the 1949–1950 season. They played basketball in the Catholic Youth Organization league. From left to right are (first row) Joe Powell, Joe Spilly, Rich Killar, Jim Oliver, Joe Hamish, and Jack Biel; (second row) Rev. Louis Telegdy (moderator), Joe Leslie, John Cengel, Rich Elo, Dave Rohr, Rich Rosinsky, and Joe Gulvas (coach). (Courtesy of Joe Gulvas.)

Phillip J. Mateja played shortstop at Purdue University and batted a .355 average for three years. After graduating in 1953, he played professional baseball for 29 games. In 1954 and 1955, he played shortstop in the Army at Fort Leonard Wood, Missouri. From 1956 to 1958, He played 301 games for the Charlotte Hornets in North Carolina, a class-A affiliate of the Washington Senators, as a third baseman and averaged .272 batting. (Courtesy of Phil Mateja.)

Before graduating in 1949, Norman L. Banas earned nine letters in baseball, basketball, and football at George Rogers Clark High School in Hammond, Indiana. He played the same three sports at Purdue University for four years. He was a teacher and coach at Clark High School and Gavit High School in Hammond for 34 years. He was inducted into the Hammond Sports Hall of Fame in 1984. He also played all three sports at Great Lakes Navy for two years. (Courtesy of Ruth Banas.)

This image shows the 1955 St. John the Baptist Catholic Slovak Parish men's basketball team that played in the Whiting Community Center. From left to right are (first row) Joe Gulvas, Jim Vrabel, Don Vrabel, and Bill Figler; (second row) Bill Rapchak, Don Poppen, Tom Burosh, Joe Siska, Paul Hajduch, Jerry Kozak, and Rev. Joseph Hajduch (moderator). (Courtesy of Jim Vrabel.)

George Blanda was born in Youngwood, Pennsylvania. He played football for the University of Kentucky before playing quarterback and kicker for the Chicago Bears from 1949 to 1958. He played with the Houston Oilers from 1960 to 1966 and the Oakland Raiders from 1967 to 1975. In all, Blanda played a record-setting 26 seasons with 340 games and 943 points. He entered the Pro Football Hall of Fame in 1981. (Courtesy of the Chicago Bears.)

George Sobek graduated from Hammond High School in 1938 and was all-state in basketball. At Notre Dame, in 1942 he was an All-American basketball player. He played professional basketball for three teams and was player-coach of the Hammond Buccaneers. He was inducted into the Indiana Basketball Hall of Fame in 1980. He played baseball for the Chicago White Sox minors for three years and managed for six years. He was a high school athletic director and baseball coach for 26 years. (Courtesy of Chip Sobek.)

John Blasko was inducted into the Greater Calumet Area Bowling Association (GCABA) Hall of Fame in 2010. Blasko has been the GCABA manager for 11 years. He started bowling at age 15 and set pins at the Whiting Community Center as a boy. Over the years, he has captained many teams. He continues to bowl in three leagues each week. He was named GCABA Officer of the Year and Director of the Year twice. (Courtesy of John Blasko.)

Stan Mikita was born on May 20, 1940, in Slovakia as Stanislav Guoth. He moved to St. Catharines, Ontario, Canada, as a young boy to escape communist-controlled Slovakia. His aunt and uncle adopted him and gave him their surname, Mikita. After three starring junior seasons with the St. Catharines Teepees of the Ontario Hockey Association, Mikita was promoted to its parent club, the Chicago Blackhawks, in 1958. The Hawks won their third Stanley Cup in 1961. Mikita became one of the most-feared centers of the 1960s. Using his innovative curved stick, he was one of the game's best face-off men. He led the league in scoring four times in the 1960s. He played for the Chicago Blackhawks for 22 years (1958–1980). He was inducted into the Hockey Hall of Fame in 1983. (Both, courtesy of the Chicago Blackhawks.)

Marian Hossa was born on January 12, 1979, in Slovakia. He plays both right and left wings. He played for Slovakia in the World Junior Championships, the Olympics, and the World Championships. Drafted by the Ottawa Senators in 1998, he was traded to three teams from 2006 to 2009. On July 1, 2009, the Chicago Blackhawks signed him to a 12-year contract for $62.8 million. He has played in five NHL All-Star games and won the Stanley Cup with the Blackhawks in 2010 and 2013. (Courtesy of the Chicago Blackhawks.)

Michal "Zeus" Handzus played center for Slovakia for 10 years in international championships. He was drafted by the St. Louis Blues in 1995 and played two and a half seasons. After being traded to two other teams, he played with the Chicago Blackhawks in 2006–2007. He was traded to the Los Angeles Kings and San Jose Sharks before returning to the Blackhawks in 2012–2013 and winning the Stanley Cup. (Courtesy of the Chicago Blackhawks.)

This is the Pearl Field Gang from the Robertsdale section of Hammond, Indiana, at their fifth reunion in 2001. During World War II, the men, who were then teenagers, played sandlot baseball at Pearl Field. Due to wartime shortages, they used patched, cracked wooden bats and taped-up balls. From left to right are (first row) J. Dolak, J. Vrabel, N. Masoles, A. Schurke, J. Strabavy, J. Fasiang, M. Koleszarik, and T. Fasiang; (second row) A. Blahunka, B. Sandrick, B. Pruzin, J. Krull, E. Matalik, S. Blahunka, A. Banas, B. Fasiang, and T. Blahunka; (third row) B. Diacek, D. Pruzin, R. Danko, D. Poppen, M. Ilianich, F. Misch, B. Drach, and N. Banas. (Courtesy of Jim Vrabel.)

The Pearl Field Gang celebrated their 12th reunion in 2009. Besides playing sandlot baseball during World War II at Pearl Field, they played touch football and ice hockey in the winter. After the war, the boys played alley basketball. From left to right are (first row) Tom Fasiang, John Krull, Steve Blahunka, Bob Figler, and Al Blahunka; (second row) Jim Vrabel, Norm Banas, Bill Figler, Joe Fasiang, Andy Banas, Bob Fasiang, and Tom Ustanik; (third row) Al Fetzko. (Courtesy of Al Fetzko.)

Nine

SLOVAK OTHER
SLOVENSKÉ INÉ

Born on September 3, 1891, in Austria-Hungary (now Slovakia), John Pavlovich immigrated to Whiting, Indiana, at the age of 19 in 1910. He married Anna Kaminsky (who was born in Whiting on February 2, 1898) on September 16, 1893, at St. John the Baptist Catholic Slovak Church in Whiting. They had seven children: Joseph, Pauline, Mildred, Irene, John, Bernard, and Betty Ann. (Courtesy of Bernard Pavlovich.)

The Slovensky Dom (Slovak Home) was built in Whiting, Indiana, in 1916. Slovak plays and concerts were performed in the auditorium that was on the second and third floors. In the 1970s, a fire destroyed the second and third floors. The American Slovak Club is now the sole occupant. There used to be a two-lane bowling alley in the basement, where pin boys would set up the bowling pins. (Courtesy of Jack Hertko.)

Johanna (Jenny) Masura from Bobrovec, Austria-Hungary (Slovakia), married Andrew Paul Ustanik Sr. from Pucov, Austria-Hungary, at St. John the Baptist Catholic Slovak Church in Whiting on April 23, 1923. Rev. Benedict M. Rajcany officiated at the ceremony. They had eight children and 39 grandchildren. Ustanik Sr. worked in the barrel house at Standard Oil Company in Whiting, and his wife was a homemaker. (Courtesy of Jack Hertko.)

Steven Blahunka Gabriella Masura Frank Gaspar & Mary Barbara Fasiang Steven Masura Jennie Ustanik
Apolonia Fasiang

On November 9, 1926, Frank Gaspar Fasiang and Mary Barbara Masura were united in holy matrimony at Holy Name Cathedral in Chicago. They grew up in the same small town of Bobrovec, Austria-Hungary; however, because of a seven-year age difference, they did not meet until adulthood. They had three boys and a girl: Robert Milton, Martha (Sr. Brigid), Joseph Rudolph, and Thomas. They had 11 grandchildren and 16 great-grandchildren. (Courtesy of Robert Fasiang.)

Men L-R: Stephen Blahunka (Groom), Joseph Masura, Jr., Kelly Pohl, John Matlon, Ferdinand Vrabec, N.A., Joseph Peters, Joseph Spilly, N.A., Joseph Pieter, Joseph Klen

Stephen Joseph Blahunka married Apolonia Caccilia Fasiang on February 13, 1928, at Immaculate Conception Catholic Slovak Church in Whiting, Indiana. Rev. John Lach performed the wedding ceremony. The couple had three boys: Stephen Anthony, Alfred Joseph, and Theodore. Stephen Blahunka was a bricklayer at Standard Oil Company in Whiting, and his wife was a homemaker. They had 11 grandchildren and 23 great-grandchildren. (Courtesy of Steve Blahunka.)

119

In 1937, Joann Opat (standing behind the cake) celebrated her ninth birthday with a party attended by children from St. John the Baptist Catholic Slovak School in Whiting, Indiana. All of the children received a cupcake with a single candle in the center. On the right of Joann is her brother Fred Opat. (Courtesy of Sr. M. Brigid Martha Fasiang, SSCM.)

Dr. Peter P. Hletko was born on June 26, 1902, in Chicago. He attended St Michael the Archangel Catholic Slovak School in Chicago, St. Procopius College in Lisle, Illinois, and DePaul and Loyola Universities in Chicago, earning his doctor of medicine degree. He married Anna Remijas on March 27, 1938, at St. Michael the Archangel Catholic Slovak Church. He served as president of the Slovak League of America and supreme medical examiner of the Slovak Catholic Sokol. He was also involved with many other Slovak organizations and groups. (Courtesy of Geri Hletko.)

On a hot summer day in 1938, Slovak families enjoyed ice cream bars at a picnic in Forsythe Park in Whiting, Indiana. From left to right are (first row) Loddy Lissy, Steve Blahunka III, Elinore Lissy, Joe Fasiang, and Tony Lissy; (second row) Ted Blahunka, Betty Hertko, and Alfred Blahunka; (third row) Steve Blahunka II, Apolonia Blahunka, Gaspar Fasiang, Barbara Fasiang, Joe Stanek, and Anna Lissy. (Courtesy of Robert Fasiang.)

This photograph from 1939 shows Charlie Shimala and an unidentified friend in front of Shimala's original grocery store and meat market in Whiting, Indiana. Fifth- and sixth-grade boys were paid 25¢ plus a 5¢ candy bar to go house-to-house passing out handbills with weekly grocery sales. The store opened in 1935 and closed in 1971. The original store was renovated. (Courtesy of Robert Shimala.)

During World War II, Slovaks from Chicagoland purchased more than $800,000 in US War Bonds to help pay for the Liberty ship SS *Milan R. Stefanik*. Under the auspices of the Slovak League of America, the total $6 million pledged by Slovaks across America was more than doubled. The ship was launched on September 27, 1944, in Baltimore, Maryland. Milan R. Stefanik was a Slovak patriot who served as a general in the French Armed Forces during World War I. He served as the first minister of war of Czecho-Slovakia in 1918 and 1919. (Courtesy of Steve Blahunka.)

The Chicago District of the Slovak League of America sold $1.6 million in US War Bonds to pay for three Flying Fortress B-17 bombers during World War II. In January 1945, the three bombers were named the *American Slovak I, II,* and *III*. The commanding officer of the Army Air Forces accepted the bombers from the Bond Drive committee chairman Dr. Peter P. Hletko. A champagne bottle broken over the bomber was given with the wishes for good speed and happy landings. (Courtesy of Steve Blahunka.)

This wedding photograph shows Marie Pardek Dubec and John S. Dubec. They were married on June 14, 1947, at St. John the Baptist Catholic Slovak Church in Whiting, Indiana. The bride was born in Slovakia and came to the United States at age 11. (Courtesy of Marie Pardek Dubec.)

A 20-year (1928–1948) jubilee celebration of the weekly Slovak parish news *Osadne Hlasy* took place in Chicago. The final year of publication of *Osadne Hlasy* was 1979, one year after the golden anniversary. From left to right are (first row) Fr. John P. Rondzik (pastor of Assumption of the BVM Catholic Slovak Parish in Chicago), and Karolina Tylka; (second row) Michael S. Rehak (master of ceremonies), Dr. Peter P. Hletko (contributing editor), Florian V. Tylka (editor), and Vendelin J. Tylka Sr. (business manager). (Courtesy of Vendelin Tylka Jr.)

Frank Paunicka (left) is the able assistant to his father, Louis Paunicka Sr., at the corner butcher shop and store in Robertsdale (Hammond), Indiana, in 1949. The store was built in 1929 and the business closed in 1963. As the cases on the floor show, pop came in glass bottles then. (Courtesy of Frank Paunicka.)

Boy Scouts from Troop No. 204—sponsored by the Holy Name Society of St. John the Baptist Catholic Slovak Parish in Whiting, Indiana—are seen camping in canvas tents in 1949. The boys were at Indiana Dunes State Park near Chesterton, Indiana. Assistant Scoutmaster Bob Fasiang (left) and Scoutmaster John Jancosek are standing in the third row. The scouts enjoyed swimming in Lake Michigan. (Courtesy of Robert Fasiang.)

Slovak bricklayers Joseph Fasiang (left) and Gaspar Fasiang are building a house in Whiting, Indiana, in 1950. Many bricklayers in Whiting and Joliet, Illinois, came from the village of Bobrovec, Okres Liptovsky Mikulas, Slovakia (then a part of the Austro-Hungarian Empire.) After sixth grade, the last year of school, many young men from this village left the farms and went to learn the bricklaying trade and work in large cities, such as Budapest, Bratislava, and Vienna. (Courtesy of Robert Fasiang.)

In 1978, John Geffert Sr., the owner of Geffert Hardware Store in Whiting, had 27 years of business experience. From left to right are younger brother Raymond Geffert, son Greg Geffert, and John Geffert Sr. (Courtesy of Raymond Geffert.)

The Rev. John J. Spitkovsky District of the First Catholic Slovak Union (Jednota) has displayed a Slovak Christmas tree at the Museum of Science and Industry in Chicago since 1995. The tree is trimmed with crystal and handmade ornaments, apples, salonky, candles, decorated gingerbreads, pinecones, and nuts. The crystal ornaments and crèche were made in Slovakia. The Slovak village, train, and tree skirt were made by Slovak tree committee members. (Courtesy of Barbara Fayta.)

Fr. Jeff Small from St. Stephen Catholic Slovak Parish in Streator, Illinois, along with five altar boys, blesses the house of Bob Elias in February 1995. The annual Slovak tradition is also to write with chalk, on the inside molding above the front door, the first two numbers of the new year, the initials "+ G+ M+ B+", and the last two numbers of the year. GMB are the initials of the three Magi: Gaspar, Melchior, and Balthazar. (Courtesy of Bob Elias Sr.)

Slovak barber Jerry Bobos cut hair at this barber shop in Whiting, Indiana, from 1976 to 2000. He worked as a barber from age 25 until he retired at age 65. For the last 12 years of his career, he cut hair part-time while also working as Hammond City Clerk. In 24 years, men's haircuts went from $2 to $10. He retired to Las Vegas, Nevada, leaving behind four sons, one daughter, eight grandchildren, and one great-grandchild. (Courtesy of Diann's Hair Affair.)

Baran Funeral Home on 119th Street in Whiting, Indiana, was built in 1938 and enlarged in 1958. The original A.L. Baran and Sons Funeral Home was founded in 1908 on Schrage Avenue in Whiting. In 2008, it was in its third generation of family ownership, continuing its tradition of compassion and commitment. (Courtesy of Robert Fasiang.)

Visit us at
arcadiapublishing.com

www.ingramcontent.com/pod-product-compliance
Lightning Source LLC
Chambersburg PA
CBHW050554110426
42813CB00008B/2357